The Folklore
of Management

The Folklore
of Management

CLARENCE B. RANDALL

John Wiley & Sons, Inc.

New York • Chichester • Weinheim • Brisbane • Singapore • Toronto

This text is printed on acid-free paper.

Copyright © 1959, 1960, 1961 by Clarence B. Randall
Copyright © 1997 by John Wiley & Sons, Inc.
Published by John Wiley & Sons, Inc.
Previously published by Little, Brown and Company, 1961.

Library of Congress Cataloging-in-Publication Data:

ISBN 0-471-18511-6

Printed in the United States of America

10 9 8 7 6 5 4 3 2 1

Foreword

WRITTEN more than thirty years ago, the chapters which make up *The Folklore of Management* ring as true today as in 1961. Mr. Randall's farsighted predictions have proven amazing perceptions of the excesses and dangers of the free market system.

In 1997, among all the fads and fashions of management books, the basic *common sense* of this book stands out as a beacon on running a business. With his lively sense of humor, Mr. Randall reveals the elements of success as well as failure in the corporate world. The *simplicity* of this book contributes to its greatness.

The Folklore of Management truly lives up to its distinction as a "Management Classic" which deserves the attention of every business person in the 1990s. Issues such as overcompensated executives, the importance of human resources, and the danger of employee overspecialization are explored in a straightforward, no-nonsense style.

Mr. Randall certainly knew how to make an effective point, and here he conveys each one with a punch. He presents one basic idea per chapter in a frank, readable style, using the simplicity which works so well for this subject matter. Each "myth" is thought-provoking, insightful, and most of all, timely.

My favorite chapter is "The Myth of the Organizational Chart." Throughout my years as CEO of Nucor, if there's one thing I've learned, it's to refrain from placing too much emphasis on the corporate organizational chart. Mr. Randall states that inflating the importance of any structural chart (or any employee's place in it) often takes away from the overall goal of the organization. I love the comment that "not even the ten commandments undertook to do more than establish the general guidelines of conduct"—a message for all those who think every corporate policy is cast in stone, and particularly for those who insist on micromanaging their business.

Many books on management have come and gone since this was written. This one has survived because this wise and thoughtful man compiled the simple truths about business philosophy and explained how each lies at the foundation of every successful enterprise. Clarence Randall surely was a man before his time.

F. Kenneth Iverson
Chairman
Nucor Steel
Charlotte, North Carolina
January 1997

Contents

Preface

WRITING A book is a great adventure, provided you can live through it.

For most of us mortals it is a slow and pedestrian process.

This little volume, for example, was sixteen months in the making. I started off with a rush when the genial editors of *Dun's Review* flattered me by asking me to do a series for them to be called "The Folklore of Management." The first article was done in short order. And the second was no particular problem, for it began to form in my mind before the first was finished. But gradually the complexity of life began to move in on me, and the monthly deadline became more and more threatening. Once committed, however, there could be no turning back, and what helped was that as the months went along I suddenly discovered that I was enjoying the whole process hugely.

Shaving was of great assistance. Nothing so stimulates the flow of ideas as does the frantic whir of an electric razor applied shortly after rising.

And no atmosphere is so congenial for utter frankness as the solitude of a hotel room late at night. Most of this writing was done at the end of a long day in Washington, and when you have had dinner and come back alone to your room, you have only two choices. You must either read a book, or write one. Finally between those two there can be but one course. Whoever tries the first will inevitably wind up with the second.

Since half the hotel rooms in the country are occupied each night by businessmen who are away from home, I wish that more of them could be persuaded to try this device, for the story of business is not being well told.

As a group, we are singularly inarticulate — in public, that is. Put a few of us together around a luncheon table and we have plenty to say. We damn the government, tell off our competitors, complain about the professors, and display generally a lively desire to reorganize everything around us. But when it comes to spreading all this on the record, so that everyone may know what we think — we just don't do it.

So it comes to pass that everyone writes about business except businessmen. Scholars who have never managed anything propound theories of management. Economists who have never had to face an annual meeting of stockholders describe the damage that we are doing to the economy. Politicians flog us and thus get elected, and labor leaders regale their membership by reciting the catalogue of our sins. But we, who know most about the subject, stand mute.

To the extent that we have weaknesses, as of course we have, we ourselves should be the ones to expose them, for by so doing, by confessing error, we would not only advance on the road toward their correction, but we would at the same time do much to restore public confidence in the integrity of our purposes.

Obviously, the best time of all for a businessman to express publicly his personal philosophy is when he has reached the senior years. It is then that his total experience can be brought into full focus, and be seen in full perspective.

Retirement is like a high plateau to which the horseman has ridden alone. Withdrawn from the crowd, he can look back calmly at the familiar scenes, and re-examine them as they stand out in sharp relief.

Gone, too, are all the old inhibitions. There is nothing that he is striving for, nothing that he fears. There is no one whom he can damage by anything that he says except himself, and so he lays every word right on the line.

He is writing for himself, and not the reader. He knows that not many people will buy his book, and he doesn't care. What he really is after is to get his own thinking straightened out, and since he knows that he cannot fool himself he says precisely what he thinks.

But there is one caveat which must be recognized. The businessman who decides to write a book is not choosing the path to popularity among his old friends. When he speaks frankly, as he must, not all of them will like what he says. They will point out to him sharply that criticism from outside is to be expected, but that it should never come from within the lodge itself. Even when they know that what he says is true, they do not like to have such things said by one of their own. They mark him down as a renegade.

Yet the hot flame of self-searching, inward-directed criticism is precisely what American industry most urgently needs in this period of world crisis. Private capitalism, private initiative, and the entire concept that is involved in the unsatisfactory term "free enterprise" is on trial for its life before the court of world opinion. The vast hordes of new world citizens whose power may in the future so greatly overbalance ours have not yet decided whether they like our way of life or not. They are watching our every move with sharply critical eyes, and American business must put its house in order, and keep it in order, if what we are now privileged to enjoy is to survive at all. The issue is just that simple, just that direct.

So I have pulled no punches in this book, and writing in that vein I have been most fortunate in my editors. They have given me the most forthright encouragement all the way.

And my cup is overflowing in that my new friends at Dun & Bradstreet and my old friends at Atlantic–Little, Brown, have joined to make this book possible.

To them both my deepest appreciation!

1

The Myth of
Communications

*U.S. business has embarked on an orgy of
communications with workers, with stockholders,
with customers, and with the general public.
Infatuated with the sound of its own voice, it
often forgets that fine words are futile unless
they are backed by corporate performance.*

A N IRRESISTIBLE urge to communicate has seized American industry.

We communicate constantly, on an infinite variety of subjects, to all who will listen — and to many who don't. We have at our command an infinite variety of media for the dissemination of our messages, and we miss no opportunity to grab the public by the lapel and pour forth some pronouncement.

This phenomenon is quite new, as measured by my own years of service in industry. Whether or not he actually said it, Mr. Vanderbilt's "The public be damned" has survived as a legend because that phrase did aptly portray the attitude of earlier business leaders. There really was a time when management cared not at all what anyone thought, and that is the origin of many of the problems that have plagued us since.

3

Now, we are extremely sensitive and self-conscious. We care what *everyone* thinks, and that is as it should be. The sole question is whether the things we say with such proliferation are wise and true; or whether we are so bewitched by the fabulous new means available to us that we communicate just for the sake of communicating and let ourselves descend to mediocrity or even deceit in our utterances.

When S. F. B. Morse, seated in the Capitol at Washington on May 28, 1844, tapped out the first telegraph message to his partner, Alfred Vail, in Baltimore and, quoting from the Old Testament, said in awe, "What hath God wrought?", he spoke in advance for all subsequent inventors. He offered this new miracle of technology as a device for the transmission of thought; at no time did he claim that it was a substitute for thought. Electronics notwithstanding, in the realm of ideas and of conduct we are right where men were in Plato's day. No marvel of science can change the fact that what a man says should be wise and true.

Reflect upon the various segments of society before whom modern mananagement assiduously presents its views.

First comes the customer. At the top of our voices, we cry our wares. Our power of amplification is incredibly increased, but the function is the same as that of the first Arab who raised his voice in the earliest bazaar. We should ask ourselves searchingly whether our morality has increased over his in the same ratio as has our technology.

Next comes the worker. We tell him earnestly and repetitively that his interest parallels ours and that what we do is well calculated to raise his standard of living — but we need to know whether, within his own frame of reference, he can accept our statements as reflecting full integrity of purpose.

Then there are the junior officers and the white-collar staff to whom we explain in fulsome language our company policies and objectives in the hope that their efforts will become more meaningful. Against these lofty sentiments, we need to measure our daily conduct as observed by these employees at close range.

After these come the stockholder, whom we exhort to enter more fully into the responsibility of ownership in return for the benefits which he receives. Are we sure, however, that we always carefully distinguish between his interest and our own interest?

There is also government, at every level — local, state, and national — to whom we freely offer advice, but more particularly, criticism. To point out the faults of office holders is our very special prerogative, but not always do we pause to ask ourselves whether

5

in managing we consistently place the public good above the expediency of corporate aims.

Finally comes the general public, among whom we single out for individual attention particular groups such as the clergy, the educators, the housewives, and the ubiquitous man on the street. On the screen of their consciousness we endeavor to throw the corporate image of our company, sometimes before we have brought it into sharp focus for ourselves.

To discharge fully the responsibility which is placed upon management by this compelling new urge to communicate and to measure up to the challenge presented by the multiplicity of the amazing new media requires a clarity of mind and a singleness of purpose which not all businessmen possess. Any company with money can command the full galaxy of communication media, but no amount of money can buy the wisdom and the integrity demanded for their use.

Take the customer. Advertising is the very lifeblood of the free enterprise system. To stimulate desire is to increase total effort and thus bring to pass the expansion of our economy. But to promise one product through advertising and deliver another of inferior quality or with an undisclosed price component is sheer chicanery.

Or, take the worker. Here, in the most realistic sense, actions speak louder than words. No amount of glittering posters on the plant bulletin boards can establish a sound relationship between the employer and the employee if safety conditions are bad, if segregation is practiced, if pay scales are below standard, or if the town is a bad place in which to bring up children.

Effective communication with officers and staff inevitably suffers when management fails to sense that in a free society a man good enough to make a strong contribution is good enough to have his own scale of values, and that the goals which he has established for the total achievement of his own life are not necessarily parallel with those which management has proclaimed for the company. Only when an intelligent effort is made to recognize and appreciate his objectives and to integrate them with those of the company, so that a high measure of self-realization is achieved through effort for the company, does communication with him become a significant exercise.

As for the stockholders, our conduct sometimes belies our professed intentions and dilutes the effectiveness of our efforts to communicate. We entice them to the annual meeting with every blandishment at our command — entertainment, food, free samples of product, plant visitations — in short, everything except clowns and can-can dancers. But when it comes to the exercise of the prerogatives of ownership, we deny them the privilege. We ask them to submit their proxies in advance, appointing us as their agents, and then, when they are sitting in their chairs, eagerly awaiting their sole chance for the year of really behaving as owners, we ask them to let their proxies stand so that we may sign the ballots for them. We do not vouchsafe them the opportunity of making even one little cross on a piece of paper once a year in token recognition of the fact that we work for them.

As for the government, we hardly communicate at all in our own right. We turn all that over to our trade association. That organization maintains a man in Washington or at the state capital who distributes an incredible number of martinis, calls all the Senators and Representatives by their first names, and bores everybody. He can hardly do otherwise, for he has no precise policy to communicate — only the lowest common denominator of opinion.

The earnestly patriotic man in public life — and there are many — really wants to know what the businessman thinks on the great issues, but he seldom gets a chance to talk with him face to face. Unhappily, too often the businessman back home doesn't even know his name. Instead, he reads the weekly trade association bulletins with great zest and feels that he is right on top of the legislative situation.

When it comes to the public, the test of the effectiveness of our urge to communicate lies in the extent to which we share the total experience of our fellow citizens and the way we ourselves behave as members of the public. If we establish leadership on a basis totally dissociated from our business, then people will listen to what we say on management problems. But if we come before them solely as special pleaders for our own self-interest, they will turn deaf ears toward us.

The principal reason why the executive who is enamored of the paraphernalia of communication doesn't really get inside the people he is trying to reach is that he delegates too much of the job. Busy with plans and projects and cost estimates, he expects his professional staff to perform miracles for him, but he himself gives little time to thinking through the whole meaning of what he is seeking to accomplish.

I have profound respect for those able men who give their lives to the study of human relations. But no one among them can successfully promulgate a policy that is neither wise nor true. He has no stock in trade but that which is given to him from above.

Take the ghost-written speech.

I say that if the executive cannot write his own speech, let him make none. If he is tongue-tied in public, it is because he is tongue-tied in private; he simply has nothing of significance to say.

Let him be himself at all times. Let the public know him as he is. Let him stand up and say to an audience precisely what he said to his seatmate on the 8:04 that morning or what he said to his associates at lunch, disagreeable as the results may be in terms of public relations. It is the views of the man himself the public seek to probe, not those of his script technician. In the Greek tragedies, the actors wore masks; but that time has passed. Today, our public is not easily fooled. It says, as did Isaac, "The voice is Jacob's voice, but the hands are the hands of Esau." Only the speaker is deceived. When he quotes Shakespeare or Herodotus he proclaims himself a fraud, and all that he says thereafter is appropriately discounted by those who hear him.

Should the ego of the executive be aroused, which is not altogether difficult to do, the whole effort at communication may fail. The glamor of the new media is highly intoxicating, and only cool heads can be trusted with it. The desire to be seen, the craving for status that has not been earned, the shortcut to recognition — these all play a regrettable part in the current urge to communicate, whereas the qualities which the world desperately needs from management are humility and three-dimensional virtue.

What society awaits from the business community today is a new intellectual ferment for the generation of wise policy, which will match the perfection of the media and sustain this new frenetic urge to communicate. The high tension lines are waiting and can carry a tremendous voltage, but the central power station is not operating at capacity.

The determining factor in effective communication is conviction. The authoritative voice that carries its message straight into the heart of every listener is that of the man who knows exactly what he believes. His utterance simply will not be denied, because it pours straight out from his spirit. Form does not matter. His sentences may not parse, he may commit crudities of pronunciation, his metaphors may lack polish, but people will listen with rapt attention because he believes so earnestly in his cause. No new marvel of technology will ever be able to bestow that quality synthetically upon a banal message from a man who has nothing to say because he believes in nothing.

With growing anxiety, society today demands from management the formulation of a new business philosophy, a re-evaluation and restatement of the purposes and objectives of the system of private enterprise. Our way of life is on trial in the court of world opinion. Our creed is being distorted by our enemies

11

with deliberate misrepresentation and by ourselves through default. We are not talking back. Sometimes I even ask myself guiltily whether we are capable of talking back.

This rethinking of values must begin in the heart and mind of each individual charged with forming policy. He must pause in the frenzy of his routine until he can determine just what the true image is which he wishes the public to form of his company. He must then inquire searchingly of himself whether that objective carries a full measure of responsibility in a free society and whether the effort required to achieve it by all those employed by the company is consistent with the full realization of their own personal goals as citizens of a free society.

Communications to the customer, the worker, the official staff, the government, the stockholders, and the public will function smoothly and effectively when total policy is thus conceived in terms of total wisdom and responsibility.

2

The Myth of the
Organization Chart

*If your company is run "by the book," if
the job description is more important than the
man, if organization charts take precedence
over the realities of personal relationships,
your organization is in danger of
succumbing to an all-too-common form
of creeping paralysis.*

WITH THE passing of the years, I am impressed by how different management men and management ways are today from those of the pre-bellum days when I was lucky enough to get my first job.

Not that management itself is any different. It has the same function in any generation under the free enterprise system. Its task is to plan the operation, secure the maximum effort from those who are employed by the enterprise, and co-ordinate the activities of men and machines. Only the methods and the working tools of management change.

When I began, there were still men who worked ten hours a day at stand-up desks. They wore green eyeshades and had only kerosene lamps to see by. When electric lights first came in, the single unshaded bulb hanging from the ceiling was so dim that they often wished they had the lamps back.

When these men arrived in the morning, they took off their coats and put on alpaca jackets to save the wear and tear on their sleeves. Most of them wore celluloid collars and celluloid cuffs that were attached to their shirts by metal clasps. Everyone that could had a mustache. They wrote with steel pens that were dipped in dirty inkwells. To preserve their correspondence, they made copies with a letter press and pasted the tissues in a large folio volume. Their telephone, when they had one, hung on a wall and had to be cranked by hand.

The boss, who was revered and feared as one who stood on the right hand of the Deity, was driven to work in the morning and taken home at night by a handsome team of horses and, in the summer, a surrey; in the winter, a cutter with jingling bells.

But among these strange characters were fine management men, some of the very best I have ever known. They dreamed great dreams and lived to see them come true. They turned out products in ever-increasing volume for a rapidly growing country. They made money and got ahead. They were the founding fathers of today's great industrial enterprises.

And all of this they did without benefit of organization charts.

Consider the modern counterparts of those earlier strong men.

For the most part, they now come to their executive responsibilities after many years of specialized training. Not only are they college graduates but they have also probably had graduate training at the Harvard Business School or some other fine institution. There they have studied accounting and merchandising and industrial engineering and have done case studies on all sorts of business problems. Their weakness is that, enamored of new methods and still of necessity lacking practical experience, they are prone to confuse the substance of management with its working tools. For example, they tend to disdain the use of the English language, which their forebears employed so pungently, and to adopt instead the representational means of communication. The chart thus takes on such importance in their minds that it becomes an achievement in itself instead of a means to an end.

Upon graduation, these eager young men with highly polished minds arrive in industry on the dead run. They can hardly wait to put into practice the exciting new techniques which they have mastered. When they walk into the office at nine o'clock on any given morning, they are inclined to view the seemingly disorganized state of chaos about them with some disdain.

At heart, they are very good stuff indeed, and so

they get ahead fast. It is not long before they receive substantial responsibility, and as they rise in the organization, their yen for the formalities of management persists. When at last their big chance comes, and they are near the top, they surround themselves with staffs who have been similarly trained, and the stamp of the chart-minded executive is placed irrevocably upon the institution that they serve.

Many of these bright young men who make up these new staffs mark the full break with the bold entrepreneurs of the past. They do not want to become president; they are content always to remain staff. Each one of the green-eyeshade boys secretly nursed the hope that one day he could become boss and have his own spanking team of bays, but I am not sure about their successors. Some of them seem to me altogether too ready to stick with their charts if to get the chauffeur-driven Cadillac they must take the responsibility that goes with it.

It is not, of course, the new techniques themselves that I quarrel with, but rather the distorted sense of proportion with which they are employed by some of this new breed of management men. Graphs are fine in their place, but they are not sacrosanct. They should never be lifted above the dignity of useful working tools.

A chart, as such, is an excellent thing. Whatever

clarifies thinking and brings a problem into sharp focus is a desirable medium of administration, but it is the beginning of the problem and not the solution. Decisions still have to be taken by an exercise of the will; the chart itself will not get things done.

There must be both selectivity and balanced judgment in the use of the modern management techniques, with choices made that are appropriate to the circumstances. Not all minds react to the same stimuli, for example, and there is no single means of communication which will transmit an idea to all persons with equal effectiveness.

Take blueprints. There is a time and a place for a sketch, but it can never replace the spoken or the written word for the simple reason that there are some men who can never fully comprehend a drawing, no matter how hard they try. The well-rounded management man will, therefore, be master of all the media and will use them appropriately. Above all, he will never forget that it is the idea and not the medium that is important.

There is a touch of sadism in all of us, and the particular form of petty cruelty which I used to delight in practicing was this: When a young engineer was admitted to my august presence, I would ask him a question that called for a reasoned reply. If he reached for a pad and pencil and began to draw, I rebuked him sharply and asked him to tell it to me in words. If he failed that test, I knew that for him ideas had to be expressed on a blueprint or they lacked validity, and doubts about his future rose in my mind. He seemed to be condemning himself to staff work for life.

The most virulent form of this mentality is found in those for whom the organization chart is the quintessence of management, the very end-all of industrial engineering.

In such companies, this imposing document, which is found in every desk and must be consulted frequently by all hands, is as long as the genealogical table of an old New England family and as complete to the smallest detail as the subject of nuclear fission in the *Encyclopaedia Britannica.* For a man not to be squeezed into it somewhere would be a fate worse than death for it could only mean that he was completely unknown. To be connected to only one boss on the chart, and that but by a single line, would be an announcement of inferior status. The men who have really arrived will be spider-webbed off in several directions by mysterious cross-hatching.

Should an outsider chance to see the document and should he advance into the fine print of the job descriptions which will be attached to the chart, he would wonder whether any work is ever done at all, since so much time must obviously be required for study and meditation upon what to do next and how far to go.

Now, obviously, to know who is to do what and to establish authority and responsibility within an institution are the basic first principles of a good administration, but this is a far cry from handing down immutable tablets of stone from the mountaintop. Not even the Ten Commandments undertook to do more than establish general guide-lines of conduct. They contained no fine print and no explanatory notes. Even the Almighty expected us to use our own good judgment in carrying them out.

It is not the preparation of the organization chart that I condemn, but its abuse: this blowing up of its significance to the point where guidance ceases and inhibition sets in. When men turn to it occasionally for broad indications of where responsibility lies so that confusion may be avoided among personnel, all of whom are willing and able, its force is positive. But when men fall into the habit of using it to avoid a task, of saying a pleased "Not me!" to themselves when they consult it, then its force is negative.

Warm human relationships must not be put into cold storage. Situations that are essentially fluid must not be frozen.

Production is, above all else, team play. Before a

football game, the varsity may study the sketch of a play which the coach has put on the blackboard, but they don't take the chart into the game with them. When the ball is snapped, if the tackle misses his man, the end gets him, no matter what the chart says.

So it must be in business. Each man must have a sure instinct for adjusting his effort to that of the man alongside him so that the over-all objective of the operation will be advanced. He should look at the music when he can, but most of the time he must play by ear.

I remember how shocked I was once when I went to call on the Chicago representative of a large corporation whose main office was in the East. I was a vice president of my company at the time. He was not only a senior vice president of his company but a director as well. I felt entirely at ease in deciding for my company the question before us without even telling my boss that the problem existed. But when I put it to him, he opened his desk, took out a black book, thumbed the pages for a few minutes, and said, "No dice. Home office!" With complete complacency he simply dumped the matter on the desk of a remote boss, because the book told him to. As a consequence, his company missed out on a matter of importance, for I had no intention whatever of going East to pursue it.

the Organization Chart

Good administration requires flexibility of both mind and method. The infinite variety of the changing pattern of circumstances that affect production and distribution demands it. The most precise organization chart that industrial engineers can draw will be out of date before it can be printed and handed round. A relationship which functions smoothly today may begin to show strain tomorrow because of a new development that could not have been foreseen. Men of good will who have broad understanding of what their jobs are intended to accomplish can make necessary daily adjustments when circumstances change, but there can be no slippage if the man is harnessed to a chart.

There is one further difficulty with overemphasis on the formalizing of business relationships, which is this: a chart which suits one group of persons will need revision just as often as there are personnel changes.

Jobs have no vitality of their own. They are parasites. They attach themselves to people and cling tenaciously to particular individuals, no matter what we may do. Take the man away, and the job will never be quite the same again. A relationship which functions smoothly under a particular chart and one set of job descriptions, so long as the original incumbents remain, will begin to show stress when promotion, death, resignation, or retirement intervene. No two individuals will ever bring successively to one job the same complex of strengths and weaknesses, and when a new teammate arrives, some compensating adjustments must be made by those around him. No chart can ever do this for them.

The wise management man, therefore, will follow the golden mean in using the new techniques, mastering them but never letting them master him. He will add them to his kit of working tools but will keep them in their place.

He will remember that the organization chart is a useful scaffold with which to build a house, but will know that it is not the house.

3

The Myth of the
Management Committee

*Who runs your company — the president
or a bevy of committees? Are decisions made
in time — or are they continually put
off for "further study" by "the group"?
Every business can profit from a well-run
committee system, but
keeping it within bounds is a critical test of
management skill.*

L ET'S FACE it. Free enterprise as we practice it in the United States is authoritarian in principle. One man decides.

At each step in the process of production and distribution, the will of one man is the activating force when a decision has to be taken. He speaks and others obey.

Not so in our government, however. There the founding fathers wisely introduced a system of checks and balances designed specifically to make it impossible for one man to decide. Consultation before action is indispensable to political freedom, and committees are bound to proliferate in public administration.

But not understanding this distinction, the businessman — with ever-ready invective — condemns all such procedures as unnecessary red tape.

By the strangest of paradoxes, the exact reverse of our situation is true in Russia. There the government is authoritarian to the last degree, while the system of industrial production which is evolving is beset with entangling checks and balances that we would not tolerate. The Communist plant manager who decides too much is apt to find himself wielding an ax in the forests of Siberia. He clears everything — with the Party, with his colleagues, with his employees. Much uncertainty, much confusion, much delay must result.

With all this in mind, I raise a question: Is a subtle change coming over American industry today, particularly in the large companies, of which we are not yet fully aware? It is possible that we ourselves are unconsciously moving — perish the thought — toward the Soviet pattern of industrial administration?

I ask this because of the current passion for committees. Delegation of authority to groups, as distinguished from individuals, seems to fit the new mood of management.

Committees are sprouting like ragweed. We have them for everything. There is one for engineering, one for production, one for product design, one for long-range planning, one for executive development. Soon we may have to do as Congress does and have a committee on committees.

the Management Committee

In some corporations it is now the finance committee which is the all-powerful source of authority. Sitting like the Presidium of the Supreme Soviet, it determines all questions with finality. Even if its pontifical deliberations delay a project so long that a smaller competitor meanwhile builds a new plant and starts turning out the product, no officer down the line dares to voice a criticism of the committee to anyone but his wife.

In other companies, no mere plant manager feels comfortable at getting excited about a new idea unless it originated within Production Planning. His not to reason why. If the staff is cowed, it follows that no outsider, not even the investment analyst or the senior partner of the auditing firm, can really be sure just where the actual focus of decision making lies.

Let no one think for a moment that I am advocating the elimination of committees from management. Not at all. I merely would like to see them restored to their proper function.

That function is advisory. They exist to help the boss make up his mind, but they should never be asked to do it for him. Properly conceived and properly employed, committees have great value. But when they become a refuge for cowardice and indecision, they carry great menace.

Fact-finding, for example, is a service within management which a well-selected group can perform admirably. Wise decisions can be taken only by a man who has before him all available information that bears upon the transaction, and seldom can he dig it out for himself. The gathering and proper assembly of data require time, leg work, perseverance, and often specialized statistical skill. In fact, the man who knows best how to use data may himself be quite inept at securing them.

Facts alone will not develop policy. Facts must be weighed thoughtfully. The nuances of their meaning must be brought out by the exercise of critical judgment.

It is here that the crossfire of discussion by experienced minds becomes of vital significance, and the committee is a medium by which this can be achieved. When, before establishing policy, the man who is to decide sits down with his associates and genuinely opens his mind to their analysis of the facts, he takes out risk insurance against the hazards of oversight or miscalculations.

Never, though, may he properly divest himself of that essential exercise of one man's will power which sets the production process in motion.

Knowing when to terminate committee discussion and take action is a key part of his responsibility. In the deliberations of any committee there are sure to be several possible courses of action under study, any one of which could lead to the desired result. The shades of difference are usually in the gray zone of the spectrum, not in the black and white. When this is true, it becomes far more important to select one proposal and get on with the job than it is to continue the debate in the hope of choosing the absolute best. It takes a wise man to sense this, and a strong one to end the discussion and act.

None of this need interfere in the slightest with crisp and orderly administration. It is all taken in stride by a well-disciplined, smoothly functioning organization. Thus conceived, the use of committees is a virtue.

But the misuse of this new mechanism of management can become a major vice. For the vacillating executive, the committee form of administration is heaven-sent. Beset with doubt, torn with misgiving about whether to go ahead with the plan before him, he turns to a group of his associates. He does so for the same reason that the lone elephant rushes toward the herd when he scents danger. Like the elephant, he does it with a certain amount of dignity, and juniors are flattered when the big boss seeks their counsel.

Yet the truth is that, deep down inside, he is afraid. Sooner or later they find that out. He really wants someone to make up his mind for him, and he cannot fail to reveal this by his conduct in the meetings. The high respect which was felt for him when he was inaccessible is dissipated, discipline falters, his voice loses its authority.

This instinct for the protection of the herd can motivate not only the chief, but every member of the group. The committee can become a safe refuge for the inattentive and the cowardly. No longer compelled to stand out as an individual whose knowledge and opinions are to be tested as his, and his alone, the committee member may steadily let down in his effort. Subconsciously, he convinces himself that he is the busiest man in the group. Surely there will be others who will do the advance study on the project if he is not able to get around to it. After all, it is really not his job.

Such a man keeps his neck safely tucked in at all times. "Least said, soonest ended" is his rule. Why risk taking a strong position on a proposal when there is no chance for him to improve his personal standing by doing so? Around the company the proposal will be known only as a committee matter, and even if what he said were to be the determining factor, no one would remember that very long. Taking cover is the safest course.

Because of the diffusion of authority under the

committee system, too often the total effort is less than the individual members would make if they were acting alone. One sure sign that the administrative process is slowing down is an increase in the frequency of postponements. When things reach the point where everyone at the meeting is looking for an out, someone invariably suggests that the facts are insufficient and that further study should be undertaken. Thereupon a new task force is appointed, and the conference adjourns in high spirits.

When a committee behaves this way, the weak executive does not press it. He is easily persuaded that the matter is too important to have its success jeopardized by hasty action, and readily agrees that there are some phases of the problem which need further examination before a decision can be arrived at. He feels that he has done his part by referring the matter to a good committee, and he aggressively defends the members' right to have more time if anyone presses him to press them.

Then there are the perils of procedure. Even a good committee, whose purposes are well conceived, can fail to turn in a good performance when the committee itself is badly handled.

First of all, the frame of reference must be precise. The members must know exactly what their job is. There must be no fumbling around when their work gets under way because they cannot agree among themselves as to what their target is. The safest course is to set it in writing. This requires straight thinking and good draftsmanship on the part of the executive who appoints the team, but the mere task of putting it down on paper will clarify his own mind.

Sometimes it is a prudent safeguard to let the committee members themselves examine the frame of reference and suggest changes before it is put into effect. That will serve to clarify their thinking, too, as well as to lock them into more willing acceptance of their assignment.

The selection of the right man to head the group is of prime importance. Chairing a committee effectively is an art, and a man may be a fine administrator without possessing this particular skill. Commonly the job is given to the man who presumably knows most about the subject, but this is sheer irrelevance. To play defensive center on a football team requires far different qualities from those needed by a quarterback. A man could be an expert in all phases of safety work, for example, without being able to take the top post in a group that is reviewing plant safety practices.

There is only one guide: Name as chairman the man who will make the best chairman. Conceivably he can do the job well and still know less about the subject at hand than any man in the group.

The good chairman should have a warm sensitivity to human values, and awareness of both the strengths and the limitations of his associates. He must be a good listener, with genuine tolerance for those whose opinions are the opposite of his own. He must be articulate, for at times he will have to restate ideas which their proponent has left fuzzy. He must have a lively sense of humor, a light touch that will keep things moving when they might otherwise get sticky. And he must have constancy of purpose.

Precision timing is of the utmost importance. Committee meetings must begin on time and end on time, so that the members may plan their other engagements. For the chairman himself to be late is unthinkable, and tardiness by others should be made to weigh heavily on their consciences. One hour is sufficient for any meeting if the members have done their homework — and if the chairman is a good disciplinarian. The hour the meeting will adjourn should be announced in advance, and adhered to as scrupulously as the hour it begins.

An agenda should be circulated in advance, so that the members know what they are to consider and can come prepared. The staff papers they are to read must be terse, with a good summary, and the member who tries to read them during the meeting should be made to feel he is a social outcast. For the chairman himself to open the meeting by reading parts of them aloud is a crime unthinkable. On the contrary, he must be able — without looking at them — to state the issue so clearly in his own words that all present will sense he has complete command of their content.

A good way to open is for the chairman to ask the proponent of an idea to explain it. Then, turning to a member who he suspects is in opposition, the chairman asks him for an opinion. When the contrasting viewpoints are before the meeting, he goes round the table asking for other comments. He tries to let the members volunteer their ideas if they will, but if he has to, he calls on specific persons, to make sure that no individual escapes the responsibility of putting his thoughts on record.

Ten minutes before the hour is finished, the chairman sums up the consensus as he sees it, trying to do so with complete objectivity, even though he himself may not fully agree with the conclusion. If he is challenged, he makes a suitable correction. If not, he adjourns the meeting.

Progress stems from the atmosphere within the group. The members must be persuaded to do their thinking before they come, to have their ideas in sharp focus. A tradition of crispness — which is nevertheless unhurried — must be developed. There should be no pressure from the chairman, for morale completely disappears before any posture that the committee is a rubber stamp. Yet, subtly, he must keep things rolling. If he himself dawdles, the job just never gets done.

The greatest foe to progress is the man who talks too often and too much. Fast off the mark when discussion starts, he is first to speak, and unless controlled, last to speak too. Sometimes this stems from commendable interest and enthusiasm, sometimes from his own great knowledge — and condescension toward lesser minds, sometimes just from plain lack of knowledge. To stop him without brutality takes high skill, but he has to be stopped or serious tensions will develop.

The converse dilemma is how to give courage to the timid member who really is a penetrating student of the subject, a man gifted with wise judgment but inarticulate. A word of praise from time to time, an occasional "I'd like to know what Tom thinks about this," or perhaps a telephone call to compliment him after the session are ways to draw him out.

Committees thus conceived and thus conducted can be a source of great strength in an organization.

A production force is a little like an army. The council of war is held the night before; but when dawn comes, the general does not hold a town meeting. He gives the command and the troops open fire.

4

The Myth of the
Production Wizard

*Perpetual motion, split-second decisions, and
jet-propelled personality are his hallmarks.
He can run any function of the business
better than the man he hired to do the job —
and he can't stop proving it. Sometimes he's
just as good as he thinks he is. But his kind
of management can cost a company its future.*

WHEN THE King of Libya moves about his country, the seat of government goes with him. This is not the fault of the monarch, who is an able person, but stems from the history of this new nation. So divided in interest are the various provinces that there can be no single capital. The net result is that when the King is in Bengasi, Cyrenaica has an intensive surge of administration, but everything slows down again when His Majesty and the Cabinet move to Tripoli.

We have businessmen who are like that — and it is their fault. At the plant level, they roam through the various departments all day long, bursting suddenly into an otherwise orderly scene with a gust of turbulence that creates intense activity for a brief period but leaves confusion behind when, like a strong wind, they blow out the door again. They move with swift decisive steps, but they do not move in any consistent direction. They speak rapidly and in a loud voice, but when they have left no one is quite sure what they have said.

At the presidential level, they roar into each plant or branch office in turn, determined to root out incompetence on the spot, spur the laggards to new effort, and in general whip up morale by a violent display of dynamic personality. They spend their lives in airplanes, seldom sleep twice in the same bed, and run up enormous long-distance phone bills. When in Peoria, they must keep in touch with Kalamazoo, for it wouldn't do to let the boys there slow down when deprived of their strong leadership.

Great ideas come to these men with a rush, and they see to it that no time is lost in putting them into effect. If it happens to be a question of finance, they call the bank direct, not the treasurer in the home office. If it is a new merchandising gimmick, they call the customer, not the sales manager. If it is a product change, they call the department head but not the plant manager. Action, action, action is their life. The very physical exertion brings them deep satisfaction. It is their symbol of efficiency.

Oddly enough, many of these men are, in fact, extraordinarily able. They are great individual performers. Like the boss on the construction job who can run every hoist and drive every tractor, they can often literally run every division of the company better than the man in charge. But as managers they spread chaos instead of leadership.

This singular defect is not limited to businessmen. It is found in all walks of life.

Take lawyers, for example. The real leaders of the bar have busy but serene lives. They can work hard over a long weekend if they have to, but by and large they keep normal hours, and they leave the job behind when they walk out of the office. But every large city has plenty of members of the bar who are no more than legal hacks. They catch the last car of the 6:10 every night, carrying bulging briefcases. These are the men who mistake overtime for wisdom.

Science and applied technology breed such men, too. They can and do put in prodigious hours in the testing laboratory, but ask them when their project will be finished or what they believe it will cost, and you will be dismayed at their uncertain replies. There must be a hundred brilliant research men for every one who can competently plan and administer a scientific program.

From the viewpoint of the stockholder in a corporation, the production wizard is dangerous, no matter whether the job he holds is that of general foreman or chairman of the board. It makes no difference how brilliant or versatile he may be when working alone on a particular task; when he attempts to organize and lead a group, his conduct is the direct antithesis of effective management, and no important responsibility can safely be put in his hands. Just as a matter of ordinary prudence, he is a bad risk for the company. To depend on him is like running a power plant without a spare generator. When he stops, everything stops.

I have seen quite a bit of shipping in my day, and I am certain that I would not want to be a passenger on a vessel where the captain was the only man aboard who could handle her in a storm — appendicitis can strike quickly, and all too often does. The master should be a fine figure of a man, whose mere appearance inspires immediate confidence in his seamanship. But on a well-run ship, where the crew is competent and well-disciplined, you won't be able to tell from down below whether the captain is on the bridge or not.

The fact that sickness or accident might remove them from the active scene never crosses some men's minds. They behave as though they believe themselves to be immortal, making no orderly provision for the future. When untimely disaster does overtake them, they are overwhelmed with surprise and indignation.

They never, of course, retire voluntarily. Hypnotized by the sense of their own indispensability, and having had nothing in their lives to provide challenge other than the daily routine of exacting physical activity, they hang on indefinitely unless removed by higher authority. Of course, when the No. 1 boss man himself is involved, there *is* no higher authority and creeping stagnation slowly paralyzes the enterprise as his senility advances.

Unhappily, too, the production wizard is usually unfit by temperament to select and train his successor, even if he were so minded. Strong men of his type do not ordinarily tolerate other strong men about them. They thrive on adulation, and favor the patient workhorse who asks nothing better than to worship from afar. Nor will strong men stay in an organization molded by such a leader. The independent spirits, those who have the creative spark and the will to advance in responsibility, find no satisfaction in this climate. They break away to find more congenial surroundings and greater opportunity.

Many companies hesitate to give up these colorful personalities because of the glamorous, though deceptive, quality of their activity. But in the long run, it is wiser to have surgery without delay. Far better to build upon a man of lesser talent who has a sound

45

instinct for team play than to hope for change in an incorrigible star performer.

The truth is that our great American corporations, those which are universally respected for the high quality of their achievements in every phase of their endeavors, are dominated not by men but by ideas. Quite often the names of their leaders, those who have made these organizations what they are, are scarcely known to the general public. Such corporate officers display in their lives both humility and a high sense of trusteeship. They know that men are mortal and subject to coronaries, but that what is wise and true will last a long, long time. They hedge every human risk by sharing responsibility and by building their promotional resources in depth. They cause an all-pervading business philosophy to seep down through the echelons of command until the common objectives pervade all ranks.

What are these ideas, these corporate concepts, which, when employed to inspire and guide group action, set apart the fine companies from those that merely get along?

First, there must be a clear-cut and reasoned labor policy, an attitude toward the work force which is based on justice and full understanding of the modern scene. This will not be formulated by lawyers, but will be consciously arrived at by thoughtful management after weighing law, psychology, economics, and human values. It will be held in common by all who deal with labor, and no individual will be permitted to substitute his own set of prejudices for the institutional philosophy.

If it is determined to put every job on a merit basis, without regard to creed or color, then this will be done with complete sincerity throughout the whole organization. Those who cannot carry out such a policy with honesty will be removed from the sequence of authority. If the contrary philosophy is to prevail, then the facts will be squarely faced. There will be no ducking the issue.

If management has determined that a particular plant will be operated on an open-shop basis, then the reasons underlying that policy will be made entirely clear to all concerned, and strict compliance with both the letter and the spirit of the law will be rigidly enforced. There will be no evasions or subterfuges.

If, on the other hand, collective bargaining is to be undertaken with one or more units of organized labor, the community will be made fully aware that the company accepts unionism and intends to deal with both the international and local officers in a spirit of complete co-operation.

When it comes to personnel policies involving rates of pay for hourly workers, salaries, incentives, bonuses, stock options, promotions, and advancement, the company will seek to establish a deserved reputation for fairness and objectivity. Nepotism will be eliminated. Every man will be made to feel that his continuing performance will be evaluated strictly on merit. This includes treating all alike when retirement age arrives.

So far as product and sales policy are concerned, the customer will come to know that instead of having to rely on the slick promises of one man — which may sometimes be brilliantly fulfilled, but are not infrequently forgotten or ignored — he is dealing with an organization that is consistently reliable. He will have confidence that every man who bears the name of that company on his business card will be found altogether trustworthy when he makes commitments.

Behind all of this there will be a consciously evolved business philosophy, a set of principles which will guide and govern the conduct of all who work for the company. By this I mean not only a positive code of business ethics, which is a must in any case, but an unqualified acceptance of the responsibilities created by participation in the American system of private enterprise. For example, the imperatives of the free market will be scrupulously respected. Those who sell will yield to no temptations here. They will know that whoever attempts to impose private control over prices is asking for ultimate public control. They will understand that when competition ends, the slow death of private enterprise begins. Monopoly power must rest in the state alone in a free society, and even there it is dangerous.

A corporation whose every activity is both motivated and governed by such a compelling business philosophy will at all times display responsiveness to public need. Its officers and employees will instinctively understand that the welfare of the institution and that of the community are inseparably linked. This is the responsibility of private capitalism, which must be accepted as the offset to the privilege of the pursuit of private gain. The preservation of our liberty can be achieved in no other way, for in this modern world social need will not be denied. It will be met, either voluntarily or by the ultimate compulsion of the state.

In addition to the corporate social responsibility, each employee, from the president down to the janitor and the watchman, has his own personal obligations as a citizen to discharge. He must be not only permitted but actively encouraged to carry these out strictly in accordance with the dictates of his own conscience. Here it is the complete absence of control that characterizes the management of a company which fully measures up to the highest standards.

For the corporation that is planning for the first time to go overseas, either to build a plant or to distribute its product — and there are many such these days — the basic code must be enlarged to add new principles to govern the unfamiliar problems that will be encountered. In the foreign country, both the physical and the human factors will be different. Desert heat and Arctic cold are difficult to cope with; so are language barriers and diversity of race, color, and religion. But social responsibility will still be the key. No officer or worker may be allowed to forget for a moment that in everything that he does he bears the flag of the United States. What he says and what he does may have a more important bearing upon the foreign relationships of our country than the negotiations of our ablest diplomats. Every American supervisor resident in a foreign area is the United States in the eyes of those who see him at work. Above all, the company will preserve its honor. It will never buy its way into a profitable concession by bribing the representatives of a foreign nation. The cynical cliché that "You can't do business in any other way down there" will never pass the lips of a man who really values the American way of life.

In a company that is dominated by ideas and not by men, one in which a consciously evolved business philosophy guides and governs all who have a part in the enterprise, how are its principles arrived at?

In much the same way that a man arrives at his own basic code of conduct. But the process, which is a function of education, experience, sober thought over a long period of time, and just plain character shining through, is a collective and not an individual process. Many, many minds must add bits of wisdom and experience until the mosaic of principles achieves solid strength and stability. Just as in the Anglo-Saxon system of jurisprudence, under which the common law developed as a composite of the thinking of countless judges, so the philosophy of a well-managed company reflects the highest common denominator of the judgments of as broad a group of leadership as is at the disposal of the management. No single brain, no single exercise of will can equal the distilled wisdom of a diversified group of informed minds. Decision making is the prerogative of the individual, but the forming of policy within which decision making is to operate is a collective function. The larger the number of minds that are brought to bear upon the forming of a basic philosophy, the greater the chance that it will be wise and enduring.

The best of ideas, however, must find expression through people. Only then do they come alive, and this is where leadership and example become of paramount importance in projecting into the community and the nation the basic code of principles upon which the ultimate reputation of a fine company rests. There are many men who know the right but dare not do it. They must be led into action by the bold, daring spirits who are completely unafraid when wisdom and truth are challenged by expediency. Such men are rare, but they mark for all time the dividing line between management which is truly distinguished and that which rises no higher than mediocrity. They know what they believe, and they never lower their standards.

Business responsibility in America during these difficult modern days is grave indeed. It calls for our very best in courage and discretion. We need mature leadership that is qualified both in breadth and in depth. Today no single man, however strong physically or brilliant mentally, should be allowed to run amok in management.

5

The Myth of the Almighty Dollar

*Are we too tolerant of the top man who justifies
a swollen salary with the magic word
"incentive"? Top-heavy executive pay reflects
a distorted view of human relations. Worse
still, it can dangerously undermine
public confidence in our system.*

THERE ARE fine restaurants in France where the *sommelier*, or wine steward, takes great pains to make sure that everyone knows who he is and what he does. His badge of office is always unmistakable, for it would make him most unhappy if anyone should confuse him with an ordinary waiter. And so he wears about his neck a golden chain, to which are attached his tasting cup and the other implements of his calling. Thus decorated, he moves pompously about, drawing attention to himself.

But there are equally fine French restaurants where the service is so smooth and unobtrusive that you do not know whether the solicitous man at your elbow is the *maître d'hôtel*, the *sommelier*, or just a waiter.

Both of these patterns of behavior will be found within the American business community by all who study the question of what the proper scale of compensation for corporate executives should be.

Industry has a few *sommeliers,* men who move among us ostentatiously, wearing about their necks the golden chains of too-high salaries and making lavish display with expense money. Happily, their number is small. They are far outnumbered by those whose compensation is so moderate and so obviously well-earned that it is never called into question.

And yet, unfortunately, the conspicuous misconduct of the few creates a problem which all of us who believe in the free enterprise system need to think through carefully.

Question the business *sommelier* about his excesses and he will talk of incentives. When you smile incredulously, he will say that although his tax bracket is so high that money as such means little to him, he needs a big salary because it is the only means he has for keeping score.

Well, maybe. But the public keeps score that way, too. The contrast between his "take" and that allotted to other people is so great that the common man is outraged and the whole concept of free enterprise is brought into jeopardy. When a man who plainly has enough asks continually for more on the grounds that he needs "incentive," ordinary people react in anger. Even good citizens wonder whether a society which permits this is organized on the right basis.

"What do you mean by a big salary?" such an executive asks. "How big is big?"

That is the question all of us need to come to grips with. No man can answer it by looking in a book. In a free society, it is a matter of conscience and of personal responsibility. The answer must be reached through the exercise of good judgment and good taste, in an atmosphere of humility.

But there are certain benchmarks. For example, if the chief officer's conspicuously high salary has been approved only by an inside board of directors made up entirely of men who work for him, whose whole futures are subject to his control, he has behaved badly. Unless his conduct has been subjected to the critical judgment of persons who have nothing at stake, he has not measured up to the standards required for a clear conscience.

If his salary is the largest in his industry, he should take warning. Obviously someone has to be at the top of any list, but under such circumstances he must be very sure he is right.

If his compensation is out of line with that of men bearing similar responsibilities in other industries, or far beyond the average for industry as a whole, he is vulnerable.

If he pays himself 50 per cent more than he pays

the officer next in line in his own company, another warning light should flash.

No man believes more earnestly than I that incentives and individual reward for effort are basic to our enterprise system. But incentive is one thing and avarice quite another. Let no one tell me that because a key executive has his year-end bonus increased by fifty thousand dollars he will accomplish that much more the following year. Human motivation is not so simple. If such an increase should suddenly be given to the Secretary of Defense, the business community would roar. Yet surely no single task in industry approaches in degree of responsibility the awesome burden borne by the No. 1 man in the Pentagon.

We in management do not ourselves accept this view of compensation where wage earners are concerned. We know from experience that explosive advances in the hourly rate do not pay for themselves by an equivalent increase in productivity. If human motivation could be calibrated that easily, all a company would need to do in order to double production would be to double the wages. Why then should we behave as though giving frequent large increases to company officers would bring about an equivalent forward thrust in executive effort?

It is said that oversize salaries are justified by the fact that the crushing burden of the income tax robs the executive of the fruits of his toil and incentive is destroyed. Reflect on that for a moment. There are two reasons why taxes are high. The first is that great sums are being drained out of the Federal Treasury each year to subsidize special segments of our population. The industrial *sommelier* does not wholeheartedly oppose these subsidies, in part because he is too preoccupied with his own affairs to take part in political activity, but also because he is not above getting some of them for his own company if he can.

The second reason for high taxes is that over half of our Federal budget goes for national defense. We live, unfortunately, in that sort of world. I suspect that George Washington and Thomas Jefferson would be quite startled to learn that business leaders of this generation wish to be relieved of participation in the defense of their country because the necessary taxation "reduces their incentive."

It is also said that Federal and state inheritance taxes reduce incentive because they make it hard for a businessman to provide suitably for his children. Those who say it are usually the very men who boast that they themselves started from scratch. They seem to have no confidence in their children, to be dead set on taking away from them the rich experience which they declare has been the source of their own strength.

To resist excessive and improper taxation is not only

the privilege but the duty of the citizen. To cry out against all taxation is to reject the responsibility and to cross the border of the credible into the ludicrous.

When the socially irresponsible few pay themselves total compensation many times greater than that of the President of the United States, they inevitably breed trouble for all business. The American people will not stand for it. I am not sure how it will be stopped, but I am certain it will be. The public has rebelled at business leadership before, with dire consequences. Time was when the railroads went too far in "charging what the traffic will bear," and that over-reaching wound up in regulation and receivership. The selfish arrogance of industry's *sommeliers* could spark another such revolt. For if feather-bedding is to be stopped at the bottom, it must be stopped at the top.

Actually, this phenomenon of self-indulgence in the name of incentive is merely another manifestation of the age-old dilemma of a free society: what to do when liberty degenerates into license, how to resist the abuse of freedom. Fortunately, the spectacular offenders are isolated cases. The overwhelming majority of men at the top play the game squarely. By their responsible behavior they demonstrate the fallacy of the false creed that only money can be relied upon to bring forth intensive and sustained effort.

They demonstrate, also, that our morality has made

progress in the century and a quarter since Washington Irving first coined the expression "almighty dollar" to describe "the great object of universal devotion throughout our land," deliberately using the word "almighty" to suggest that money to many Americans was next to God.

Were further proof of higher ethical standards required, it would be found in the lives of those dedicated men and women in other ways of life who give their utmost to the service of mankind for meager compensation. Grade-school teachers get no year-end bonuses, and college professors are granted no stock options. Few clergymen can remember back to when their annual stipend was last increased. Junior career officers in remote embassies rate with brick-layers in take-home pay and cannot strike for an increase. Yet most of these, and countless others like them, turn in fine performances.

Why must business be different? Is production ignoble? Is the whole activity so tawdry that ordinary human motivations do not apply? To enlist the human effort that society so urgently needs must we descend to the level of haggling for merchandise?

Not at all. I reject that concept utterly. The truly wise men at the top know that the development of a team, whether for a company or for the country, on which every member gives of his best all of the time rests upon something far finer than just dollar appeal. No one questions the principle that under the enterprise system effort must be fairly rewarded, but the thoughtful leader understands clearly that there are other incentives closer to the human heart than the pocketbook.

What are these other motives that hold men to tasks and drive them to great effort? There are many, but none is more powerful than a sense of challenge that anticipates pride of achievement.

They say that a mountaineer climbs a mountain just because it is there. That is precisely the spirit in which most men go about their jobs in business. When I hear it said that success lies in doing well that which we want to do, I disagree. Few of us are wholly free agents in the selection of our callings. I say that success lies in doing well that which we have to do, and that this in itself brings a large measure of reward.

I hold the old-fashioned, naïve view that every decent man wants to pull his weight. Being human, he likes to be told that he has done a job well — but if he is made of the right stuff he knows it already. He can be deeply hurt if he believes he is being treated unfairly in the matter of compensation, but nothing moves him so profoundly as the inner satisfaction that comes to him when he can honestly say to himself, "That was a good job."

Wise management builds on these principles. Every member of the team is given a chance to understand the full meaning of the goal and of the part he has to play, so that he may judge his own performance before the returns are in. He is made to feel that what lies within his sphere of activity presents an opportunity for significant contribution to the total effort, and that the extent of his addition to the whole will be objectively appraised. In making the effort, he is not counting on the pay increase, because he is accustomed to an atmosphere of fair dealing.

A trained seal blows the trumpet because the man in the center of the ring throws him a fish. He got it the last time. That leads him to think he will get it this time.

But the good worker in our country — and by that I mean not only the crane operator and the shipping clerk but the president of the company as well — blows the trumpet because he likes to blow. He hopes to go on eating, but he isn't thinking about that whenever his turn comes to perform. He blows his best anyway.

6

The Myth of the
Magic Numbers

*To cash in on the businessman's present
preoccupation with surveys and
factual summaries, a rash of new service
organizations has sprung up which will
study anything for a fee. The vacillating
executive turns to them eagerly.*

THE DYNAMIC power which drives our American economy forward is freedom of choice: freedom to buy or not to buy; freedom to spend or to save; freedom to work or not to work; freedom to risk for gain; freedom to follow a fresh impulse wherever it may lead. The outward characteristic of this economy is continuous and unforeseeable change. This is the quality which differentiates it from one controlled by the state. A static society is expected to perform steadily. One which draws its spontaneity from innumerable individual actions cannot possibly have a predictable pattern.

The supreme test of good industrial management in today's America is its resolute capacity for swift adjustment to change. Revolution follows revolution in technology. Science advances with such disconcerting speed that by the time basic research has found expression through applied research and a new product appears on the market, the basic concept may itself have been superseded. With the long lead-time which our complex mechanisms require before coming off the manufacturing line, the new end-product may be obsolescent before it reaches the customer. Developments that are far from scientific have an equally unsettling impact upon industry. Subtle variations in taste and demand appear in a flash — to vanish as quickly. The necessities and luxuries of today become the discards of tomorrow.

Social values alter, too. What is respected or coveted today as a symbol of status may fall tomorrow under the ban of an unforeseen taboo. Style preferences, rising standards of living, fear of war, class animosities, geography, new means of transport — all these factors and many more strengthen demand in one quarter and weaken it in another, with the result that levels of production are constantly threatened by uncertainty.

The only constant in the equation of industry is change itself. As each such disturbance strikes our economy, new challenges confront industry and new decisions must be taken. The formula which resolved the previous crisis may prove futile this time. There must be a continuous reorientation of outlook, a continuous redevelopment of management effort on new fronts.

Regardless of heavy loss, product lines may have to be redesigned swiftly to reflect advanced techniques. New marketing areas may have to be sought overnight and rapidly exploited. Plants may not only have to be rebuilt but relocated. Sources of raw material never before used may have to be found. The transformation can be so sweeping in its effect that the whole corporate and financial structure of the company has to be overhauled.

In the midst of such turmoil there is little time for sober thought and many a harassed executive loses his head. He yields to mob psychology. His first thought is to ask what his competitor is doing. A hasty readjustment program, conceived on a crash basis by one company, can sweep through an entire industry.

It is at such times that businessmen begin to play the numbers game. The timorous and hard-pressed executive, who deep down inside resents and resists change, abandons the realm of ideas and individualistic, creative action. He seeks refuge in statistics. Not sure of his own thinking, and hesitant to plunge boldly ahead on a plan of his own that would put his personal status in hazard, he takes protective covering in conformity with whatever general level of conduct seems to be emerging.

His first step is to order a survey. He does this under the plausible pretext that he must ascertain the facts before reaching a decision, but actually he is seeking reassurance drawn from the law of averages. It is both easier and safer to follow the rest. And since many of the rest will be behaving in exactly the same way, a colorless format of unimaginative uniformity can envelop an entire segment of our economy, solely for lack of leaders who have the courage to dig beneath the statistics and evaluate the imponderables.

We survey everything these days. Myriads of little men and women, equipped with sharp pencils or recording devices but lacking in sufficient understanding of the problem to form sound judgments, are sent out to ask innumerable questions of all comers.

Today we ask the consumer what he intends to buy, regardless of whether he has given the matter serious thought and often at a time when he couldn't care less. We ask the worker what he finds wrong with his job, with perhaps no better result than to activate his natural human instinct for dissatisfaction. We ask directors what they propose for capital expenditures in the ensuing year, and by asking strengthen their uneasiness over spending at all. We ask the business leader what he sees for the immediate future, knowing that he cannot know — and we do it at a time when he himself is awaiting the result of a survey that will tell him what to think. The net result is that the courage and insight of wide, experienced minds is swallowed up in the accumulated mediocrity of the thoughtless and the irresponsible.

The men of the press, who are incurably pattern-minded, and whose hasty judgments often tend to submerge the particular in the general, have helped to lead the public into practicing this numbers game. They are incredulous when an executive speaks out against a trend, much happier when he confirms the story which they have written in their minds before the interview. They have induced investors to rely on the averages in determining when to buy and when not to buy, instead of practicing discrimination by bringing a particular security, and it alone, under careful examination.

They have imposed upon the steel industry the inexorable and unfair formula of capacity as a measure of performance. For the welfare of the economy it is tons shipped out that count, tons for the current period as compared with tons for a representative period. Capacity deals only with readiness to serve, and the question of whether it is too large or too small is totally unrelated to the soundness of the immediate general level of the economy.

71

There is one thing to be said on the credit side, however. The press and the pollsters have overreached themselves. In their professional enthusiasm for the significance of surveys, and their aggressive insistence that they are exercising a right, not a privilege, they have started a sharp public reaction against their techniques. The American people are getting annoyed at having their privacy invaded so incessantly by the little men and little women who ask questions. At first they were intrigued and amused. Now they are bored and petulant. They solemnly give phony answers, and have a hearty laugh after they have closed the front door on the survey taker.

To cash in on the businessman's present preoccupation with surveys and factual summaries, a rash of new service organizations has sprung up which will study anything for a fee. The vacillating executive turns to them eagerly. If, for example, he has a salary problem or is troubled at how large the incentive bonuses should be, these repositories of all useful knowledge will promptly send him an impressive dossier. They will show him at a glance just what the controller receives in compensation, both regular and extra, in the A, B, and C companies, and so on down through the alphabet. If he would use these tables only as a check, one tool among many, still relying on his own judgment, all would be well. But when he blindly accepts the average as conclusive, he betrays serious weakness. No two companies are alike, and no two controllers. Duties and abilities vary widely, and it is the particular, not the general, that is important.

All such ready-made averages necessarily reflect large, undisclosed areas of incomplete data, for they are based on returns from only those companies that elect to co-operate. Understandably, many well-managed institutions think it improper to reveal such information to outsiders, however well intentioned, and the consensus may in some cases represent the views of other vacillating executives who have themselves followed earlier tables. Faulty judgment can thus be compounded and continued indefinitely.

In labor circles, and in some of management as well, the cost-of-living index is the supreme sacerdotal symbol. As statistics go, that particular figure is probably arrived at with as much care and technical skill as any in current use. But when all is said and done, it is at best only an average that glosses over particularity with a heavy layer of generality. Quite apart from the fact that the cost of living when used as a basis for increased wages is unsound economics, unless associated with increased productivity, the use of the index on a countrywide basis is manifestly unfair. It penalizes some workers and overrewards others.

Quite obviously it costs more to heat a house in Duluth than it does in Phoenix, oranges are cheaper in Miami than in Chicago, and milk is more expensive in the coal-mining districts of West Virginia than it is in Wisconsin.

Even our learned friends in the universities have made their contributions to the numbers hypnosis, but at least they have had the grace to confess error. Sociologists now know that they cannot express the inscrutable factors of human motivation by simple formulae. For the most part, people still do what they do for reasons known only to themselves. Educators frankly admit that the Intelligence Quotient, worshiped for so many years, measures merely the ability of the mind to absorb and retain facts. It cannot reliably indicate which young men possess the vital qualities of creative imagination and leadership.

Electronics has made its contribution to the numbers hypnosis. When, by pressing a button, it is possible to turn up the names and addresses of all red-haired customers in cities of ten thousand population throughout the United States, the temptation is great to believe that by building larger machines and adding to the array of buttons there is almost no problem that cannot thus be disposed of.

We have gone through periods like this before. Susceptible as it always is to the infection of crowd psychology, the business community has raced after false gods in other days. Time was when Technocracy was the thing, but happily that particular bit of madness passed into oblivion almost before the printer's ink was dry on the pages of the books that proclaimed it. And then there was the furor over organizing industry along "engineering lines": a few would manage, and all others conform to plan without the inconvenience of taking thought. (It was never quite revealed how those who were to manage and those who were to be managed would be selected early in life, but the concept met the early demise that it merited.) Engineering counts when it comes to putting rigidity into buildings; the exact opposite is required in human relations.

But the most depressing aspect of the numbers mania is that it results in the exaltation of the average. The discriminating search for the superior and the excellent in all things is forgotten.

What difference does it really make, for example, what the average man thinks about anything? If he is the median, he is not a leader, and it is the man out front who must take America ahead. Perhaps we should know the average man's opinion so that we may be alerted to our weaknesses, but society needs to follow the best, not the second best. To poll ten people on a street corner about the outflow of gold is to wallow in trivia. We need, instead, consuming zeal for the cult of the distinguished — in ideas, in minds, in character, and in leadership.

There are no shortcuts to wisdom that bypass thought and judgment, and industry would be well-advised to abandon its search for yardsticks, rules-of-thumb, and ready-made answers. An executive who is unwilling to stand or fall on his own evaluation of circumstances and his own decision betrays weakness. Implied in the whole of our educational processes and our free way of life is an emphasis on the signficance and the particularity of individual choice. Whatever tends to glorify the average ignores the steady onward momentum of that national characteristic. Resort to the concept of the average in business must in the long run be self-defeating, for consumers soon will refuse to deploy, workers will not goose-step, and those thinking members of the general public who really form opinion, though often lamentably inarticulate, will in the end have their way.

Studies and surveys are only guides: they are not tablets of stone handed down from the mountaintop to embody eternal truth.

7

The Myth of the Specialist

*Unless the danger is seen in time, galloping
specialization can bring any company
to the brink of chaos. The remedy? Top
managers with the breadth of vision only
a liberal education can provide.*

IT IS recorded in the Book of Exodus that when Pharaoh hardened his heart Moses came in unto him, and speaking for Jehovah, said:

"If thou refuse to let my people go, behold, tomorrow I will bring the locusts into thy coast. And they shall cover the face of the earth, and they shall fill thy houses."

All of which came to pass. "The locusts went up over all the land of Egypt, and rested in all the coasts of Egypt; very grievous were they."

When Pharaoh saw the locusts he was frightened and repented. Thereupon Moses entreated Jehovah, who "turned a mighty west wind, which took away the locusts, and cast them into the Red Sea."

Industry today is like Pharaoh of old. We too are threatened with a swarm of locusts — but, unlike

Pharaoh, we are not frightened, nor have we repented. We have no Moses to intervene in our behalf and no west wind to blow the locusts away. On the contrary, we are urgently asking for more of them.

Our locusts are the specialists — the men who, with infinite patience, skill, and learning, have completely mastered one minuscule segment of a business and can do nothing else. The fractionalization of human knowledge which has come in this generation, driven by the powerful forces of international rivalry and commercial competition, has brought an incredible proliferation of separable responsibilities, which the specialists have swarmed in to take over. Industry cannot now live without them, but it may soon have to decide whether it can live with them.

At present the demand is growing much more rapidly than the supply. In every aspect of business, whether it be technology, finance, or marketing, ambitious management is searching out narrowly but intensively trained talent in response to the urge for ever sharper focus in the application of knowledge. With newer companies that are rapidly on the make, a prestige factor may also enter in. They want a man who not only is a master in his tiny area but enjoys a national reputation as such.

When the chase is on, the inquiry does not center around the question of the man's future potential or his capacity for acquiring new skills and abilities, but solely upon what precise knowledge he now possesses which the company can turn into quick profit.

Universities are the happy hunting grounds of these new talent scouts. Let a young professor get a burst of publicity in his chosen field and the prowlers will swoop upon him. Maybe is is a young research scientist whose Ph.D. thesis added another decimal to an equation in the electronics field, or even a sociologist who became articulate on some such subject as the impact of urban living upon incentive pay scales. The new lightning can strike any one of such.

Government, too, is a favorite stalking ground for these covetous recruiters. Many a harassed executive who is unexepectedly called to Washington has his eyes quickly opened by the experience. After sitting uneasily in his chair for a few minutes at his first conference, he suddenly realizes that the career officer on the other side of the table is extraordinarily competent — in fact, knows more about his particular problem than he does himself. "Aha," he says to himself. "Here is the very man I have been looking for. I've had enough of this grief. Let him handle it for me from now on!"

Because much of this hot pursuit of pin-point talent is the result of impulse thinking on the part of someone in management, rushing in to solve an immediate crisis, it is often indiscriminate. Neither the man's future nor the company's weighs heavily in the decision. The accent is on action.

Often, therefore, the approach to the prospect is heavy-handed. The executive who is given to rushing off on tangents of this sort is almost sure to be of the "money talks" persuasion. He goes after a brilliant young chemist in a university research center with all the finesse that the Yankees would use in snaring a bonus pitcher. Offer to double the man's pay and he will sign: that is all he knows. It would never occur to him that a scholar might be pursuing his subject solely for the love of it — that the chance to have a glorious part in once more pushing forward the frontiers of knowledge might be worth more to him than any amount of money. Nor could he sense that a career officer in government might be so dedicated that his pride in serving his country would transcend the prospect of even large monetary reward.

Such hot pursuit of special-purpose brains is likely to create more problems than it solves. The end result is likely to be frustration for the company and heartache for the man and his family.

Assimilation into the organization is frequently difficult, and a sense of common purpose is seldom easily arrived at. If the much-touted new specialist comes from a university, he may bring his ivory tower with him — and I say this not unkindly but realistically.

More often than not, the specialist has never actually been a member of a team before. Heretofore, he has always set his own goals, planned his own work, and fixed his own schedules. Now he must accept objectives that management selects, and meet management's time schedules. This comes hard, and it can start an inner rebellion that will eventually either cause him to resign, or so check his efforts that he will sink quietly into ineffectuality and oblivion.

Communication both during and after assimilation is as difficult as the assimilation itself. When the locusts descended on Pharaoh's palace there was doubtless a terrific buzzing, but no communication of ideas was taking place; each locust was buzzing to himself.

So it is likely to be with the specialists. Often they can communicate neither with each other nor with their new associates. Each speaks a characteristic patois that is unintelligible to all but his kindred spirits. So they clam up until by chance they come upon one of their own kind, when they become suddenly and explosively garrulous.

Specialists suddenly lured in from the outside are only part of the problem, however. There is a sinister tendency, also, to breed them within the organization. In well-managed companies a young man's traditional key to advancement is so conspicuously to fill his job to overflowing with enthusiasm and ability that all the supervisors who see him take notice and begin to vie with each other for the chance to promote him. Unhappily, also the converse can be true. In some companies the most tragic mistake a young man can make is to do his job brilliantly, for then he is promptly marked down as indispensable and irrevocably locked in. Callous and negligent management permits him to live out his whole life confined voluntarily in one narrow groove, simply for lack of the imagination to find another man to put in his place, and the courage to take the risk of change.

But from whatever source the specialists come, they are a threat to the oneness of purpose, and the understanding interlocking of responsibility, which every successful organization must have. Unless the danger is recognized and forestalled, myopia replaces breadth of vision, and synthesis of effort fades out. When the process goes far enough, a company can become as disorganized as an army without generals, made up entirely of sharpshooters. Unless all the varied and special skills found throughout the entire force of employees can be brought into unity of effort by minds broad enough to sense the composite value of all of their efforts, and wills strong enough to pursue implacably the main purpose of the whole undertaking, only gorgeously implemented confusion and frustration can result.

But before considering the plight of a company which is overstaffed with specialists, one might well stop and consider the plight of the specialist himself.

The intense overemphasis by an individual upon a single field of knowledge and the acquisition of one particular skill usually begins in college. It is a function of the modern trend in higher education, which in turn reflects the increasing fractionalization of knowledge, and it is in the institutions of higher learning themselves that the antidote must be found. It is not only in science and technology that the problem exists, but in the liberal arts as well. The sin can be committed in history as easily as in geology.

Educators understand this, but young men planning to enter industry do not, as a rule. Their minds are on the main chance. They want jobs, and they are still under the naïve impression that they will be hired for what they know.

They are usually too immature to sense that discerning management is much more interested in their proved capacity to learn after they will be on the job, and their courage to tackle something for which they have not been trained, than in the facts they carry in their heads.

In my own case, chance plunged me into the steel

industry without warning. Looking back from the high plateau of retirement, I am glad it happened that way. Had I even dreamed that steel might be my career, I would have concentrated on metallurgy, chemistry, mechanical engineering, and geology, and would have missed Shakespeare, philosophy, economics, prose composition, public speaking, and law. No amount of technical training, for example, would have served to help me play my part in dealing with the labor problems of my generation; but law, and learning how to speak and write the English language, did.

The young man who knows but one subject, even though he has completely mastered it, takes a frightful risk when he applies for his first job. He may be handcuffing himself into a situation where the future is limited, from which there will be no escape. He may rise rapidly at first, only to hit a ceiling which he cannot pass. Or he may have chosen a specialty that will eventually lose importance because of the changes that come in industry.

Just as a matter of sheer prudence, it would seem to be safer to sign on as a utility infielder who can play any base and hit a long ball against all kinds of pitching, than to be the best shortstop and able to hit only a pitch that is low and outside.

This may explain why a man with almost no formal education occasionally goes straight to the top in business. Because he was forced to leave school early, he values the education that he lacks more than do some that have it. He is determined to learn, and he gladly accepts whatever challenge the day brings. Precisely because he is expert in nothing, he tackles everything. He never gets tagged as a specialist. He gains breadth of experience and depth of understanding. His superiors are watching him, and because they perceive these qualities, new doors of opportunity continue to open out to him which would have been closed had he stayed in one groove.

From the point of view of the company, this modern passion for the proliferation of specialists, and the subdivision of business into watertight compartments, goes straight to the heart of sound administration. Breadth at the top cannot be built on a foundation of narrowness at the bottom. When death or resignation or retirement remove a responsible officer, his place cannot be filled by trying suddenly to make a generalist out of a specialist.

Wise and effective leadership is practiced only by those who have overcome, as far as humanly possible, all limitations of the mind. Management functions within no single frame of reference. Its scope is as wide as that of the whole operation, as broad as life itself. Whatever constricts the mind must be overcome. As the ladder of responsibility is climbed, each successive step demands more and more flexibility of intellect, more and more capacity to comprehend divergent forces, and more and more power to correlate them into a unified whole.

In the last analysis, only the man himself can correct and overcome the imbalance of performance that specialization creates. Only he can undertake and achieve the broad cultivation of the mind that brings the wisdom, the tolerance, and the intellectual fortitude which are the hallmarks of distinguished industrial leadership.

Industry, however, can play a very significant part in restoring balance if it will lift its own sights and make it clear both to educators and to students that unrelieved specialization is considered a liability and not an asset.

Changed methods and new techniques may have to be devised for college recruitment. Personnel officers must put new emphasis upon general qualities, and when choosing specialists must favor those who have demonstrated in their preparation for life a marked capacity for breaking out of the limitations which their studies have imposed.

Industry must, of course, have special skills — now more than ever. But they should be grafted onto a broad base of wide outlook and general understanding. This means that at some point in his career each ambitious young man must consciously and earnestly undertake the broad cultivation of his mind. A general education, however acquired, has become indispensable to advancement in business.

The best answer for the young man who aims high is to complete a full liberal arts course first and then go on to his chosen field of special study. The opportunities and demands for competence and talent being what they are, there would seem to be no reason why the period of his preparation should not receive as many years of effort and sacrifice as those required of a surgeon.

Where this is impossible, there are two alternatives. Either the young man graduates in the liberal arts, and pursues his specialty later on, after employment, or he reverses this, taking his specialty in college and going on to general studies after employment. The first method works better than the second, but either will do. Certain it is that from now on ultimate success in the business world will be in direct ratio to breadth of education and training.

Business must learn this: Every general should be a sharpshooter if possible, but the fact that a man qualifies as a sharpshooter is no indication at all that he can become a general.

8

The Myth of the
Cost Cutter

When profits shrink and prospects for the coming months look dim, the cry goes up — "Slash overhead!" But that is just the moment when hasty action can do irreparable harm.

WHENEVER THE American economy pauses to take a long breath, as it must and should from time to time, the thoughtless executive reaches for the panic button. Impulse thinking replaces calm judgment. A sudden rash of unreasoned cost cutting breaks out. Economies which should have been undertaken earlier, and spaced appropriately one by one, are made all at once in a disorderly fashion. Soon the alarm bell is ringing wildly, and the net result is to shove the "down" lever of the business cycle, instead of holding everything steady until the forward thrust can begin again.

Cost cutting, as such, is a very significant function of management. It is what keeps a particular business organization lean and sinewy, and it is vital to our economy if the United States is to maintain its competitive position in critical world markets.

But cost cutting should be a year-round process, continuing and orderly, repetitive and done according to plan — never a mere orgy of bloodletting. It should do for business what pruning does for the vine, the bush, and the tree.

The world around, hardy men who make their living by harvesting the fruits of the soil know when and how to use the pruning knife. They have no more useful working tool. Whether it be the French peasant who gives daily, almost hourly, care to his precious two hectares of sun-drenched hillside soil in Burgundy, or the cherry grower of Michigan, or the owner of an apple orchard in Virginia, he preserves the quality of his product by his skill in removing deadwood. The significant thing about his operation, however, is that he works at it all the time. Never does he rush out in terror to lay about him with an axe, slashing indiscriminately right and left.

He is steady and consistent about the whole process and keeps constantly at it. In a spring following a bumper crop, when he is sure that he has a vintage product, he does the same amount of trimming as after one of those sad years when the hail damage has all but ruined him.

Not so in industry. Our morale goes up and down with the sales charts. When the economy is bursting at the seams, and smoke is coming from all our stacks, we talk little about cutting costs. We put the pruning knife away in the back of the tool shed, where it rusts from disuse. We pay small attention to expense items and say to ourselves with a shrug that even if some particular item is a little unnecessary, the government is paying half of it anyway.

The fallacy in this argument is that although a business expense used as a tax deduction may help the company, it hurts the country by precisely the same amount. Someday we will realize that unless the businessman thinks more about his country and less about himself, we may not always have a country. The welfare of the whole economy is more important than that of a particular corporation, and an executive must learn to ask himself what would happen to all of industry if everyone should simultaneously act as he proposes to act.

In the old days of our clipper ship ancestors, when a sudden storm struck, all hands were sent swarming up the masts to take in sail as rapidly as possible. Soon the vessel was stopped dead, stripped to her bare sticks. There she wallowed in the trough of the seas until the danger passed and the glass began to rise again.

Industry cannot afford to behave that way in today's Soviet-threatened world. The master of the clipper ship had only the safety of his crew and cargo to worry about. We, on the other hand, have an imperative obligation to plow through the storm. We cannot let the American economy get becalmed, either. *We must make our own wind, if need be,* but it is far better to watch the weather in the first place and never let ourselves get caught carrying too much sail.

Each industrial enterprise is an inseparable part of the community in which it operates, and each community is a part of the nation. We are not free to make decisions solely on the basis of saving our own skins. The high privilege of making good profits in boom times entails high responsibility in bad times.

Each sudden cut in expenditures made by one company to protect its own position means a loss of business for someone else. In a chain reaction, retrenchment by one breeds retrenchment by another, and the collective recklessness thus produced can drive the economy as a whole into a severe depression which more responsible conduct would have avoided.

Many a wise captain has brought his ship safely to port because, knowing that storms might come, he carried adequate ballast. Financial reserves are the ballast of industry. Where there is business statesmanship and full understanding of the inevitability of fluctuations, cash set-asides are established in good times, to be spent courageously in bad. By such conduct only can we collectively mitigate the impact of pauses and recessions.

When a sudden fury of ill-considered cost slashing sweeps through a company, "We must cut overhead" becomes the slogan. Yet this mystic catch-phrase seldom means the same thing to different men. To many, it is a simple command to cut off, overnight, every expense that does not pay off at once, here and now. Hack away at the intangibles. Forget the future. Have no thought for human values. Give up planning for the long term. Stop construction. Suspend plant maintenance. Permit no nonsensical talk about that overdue paint job. Forget equipment replacements. Cut inventory to the bone, even though it means shutting down the plant of a loyal supplier. Take care of yourself, and let the devil take the hindmost, through the whole dizzy descent down into the abyss.

Advertising is a favorite target for the cost cutters. It rates as "overhead" when the non-spending spree is on, and the temptation is always strong to lop the appropriation in two. Yet a downswing is the very time when it is most urgent for a company to increase the demand for its products. The striking new phenomenon in our economy is that basic industry can be bumping along on slim schedules while consumer spending remains high. Surely such a combination

97

fairly cries out for more and better advertising instead of less.

Public relations brings another gleam to the cost cutter's eye. Only the most enlightened executives are ever genuinely excited about it, at best. When income starts to fall, there is little resistance to cutting its appropriation. Yet when the storm clouds are gathering and the financial writers are ringing the alarm bells, it is more than ever important for management to project for the company an image of creative leadership and strong social responsibility.

Charitable contributions are almost certain to be attacked. "Stop the handouts!" is the cry, as though this spending were merely a form of largesse, like throwing out gold pieces from the carriage when the earl rides through the village, instead of being the most sacred sort of civic obligation. No sensible board of directors would question the principle that such set-asides should rise and fall with corporate income, but the answer again lies in reserves. Wise management, through the establishment of a foundation, or some other fund, has the foresight to overaccrue in good times, spending less than is accumulated, so that when disaster threatens and the community need is greatest, hospitals, social agencies, and educational institutions may have a steady and continuing level of support.

The most tragic error of all is to cut off the recruitment of able young men. Someone raps out the order "No more hirings!" — and forthwith the vital flow of brains, training, and character into the organization is blocked. Back to the gas pumps with this year's graduates from colleges and technical institutions, back to mediocrity for the company's leadership twenty-five years hence — all for the sake of making third-quarter earnings look better in the current year. This is mortgaging the future with a vengeance.

Because of such conduct, the Great Depression of the early '30's laid across many fine companies a permanent blight which can still be seen as the leaders move onward in their corporate history — solely because little men with craven hearts hired no youngsters in that dismal era. It has been like the shadow of a single dark cloud that moves progressively across an otherwise bright landscape, and it will go on until those vacuum years cross the line of normal retirement.

A secondary phase of this management myopia is the sharp cutting back of all personnel training and development programs. These, too, are intangibles. They can come under the same condemnation: "Cut the overhead!" When this happens, units of physical production are given precedence over human production. Monetary necessities control human necessities, and only the years that lie ahead will reveal the heavy price paid for such shortsighted decisions. Building a sound organization is a never-ending task, and the only right time to work at it is all the time.

One serious, seldom-recognized consequence of explosive and frenetic cost cutting is the effect which it has on the people who carry on the day-to-day routine tasks. When the president goes about snapping off light switches, turns the thermostats back two degrees, or takes one bank of elevators out of operation, he breeds fear and unreasoning apprehension in the hearts and minds of everyone around the place. He magnifies the danger instead of allaying it.

It is so on a ship. When the captain gives the order to swing out the lifeboats, it does little good for him to tell everyone there is no danger. His actions speak louder than his words. Men who are afraid they will lose their jobs, or at best be put on broken time, work neither well nor safely. Rumors fly thick and fast, and what is feared becomes more deadly than what is real. Magnify this by the number of salaried and daily-wage employees in all industry and you have a national problem. It ceases to be economics and becomes crowd psychology, the forerunner of crisis.

The regrettable aftermath to irresponsible private conduct is the damage done to the basic concept of private initiative, which is under reappraisal everywhere in the world. Without the right climate, private enterprise cannot survive.

Whenever industry fails to solve a national problem on its own, government must. Social pressures mount to the point where they simply will not be denied, and no matter what political party is in power, steps must be taken to overcome the emergency. Once taken, these can never be undone. A new pattern will be permanently imposed upon our national life.

It was so with the generation ahead of ours. Management then met a downturn in the economic cycle in forthright fashion. It was direct and immediate in cutting costs, but irresponsible in terms of the disastrous effects on the welfare of the country as a whole. It simply turned half the employees loose to fend for themselves — and often this was not even layoff, but just plain dismissal. This not only jettisoned valuable accumulated skills and experience for the company. It also helped to bring into being formidable new social forces. When these pressures had been resolved by government action, there had been created an entirely new array of social mechanisms which are now a permanent part of the industrial regime — unemployment insurance, Social Security, strong labor unions, and the demand for a guaranteed annual wage.

It is conceivable that we will soon face the building up of similar powerful forces. The concept of central planning is attracting new advocates who have strident voices.

The American people are now becoming much more sophisticated in their understanding of economic matters, and searching questions are being asked which someone will have to answer — either industry itself, or government.

Industrial statesmanship is required to meet this challenge, leadership that will of its own volition, and by the use of its own resources, undertake to flatten the curves and level out the swings.

But this means constant and courageous planning in both the ups and the downs. It demands restraint and moderation at all times. We must resist both overexpansion in the booms, and overzealous cutbacks in the pauses. Like good military commanders, we must try never to occupy a forward position that we cannot defend, and we must always keep reserves that we can throw in, instead of retreating ignominiously.

Let us learn a lesson from the French peasant and his vineyard. He knows that he must keep everlastingly at his pruning in the spring if the picking basket is to be full in the fall, but he never trims off so much that he damages the vines. If a sudden hailstorm in

September ruins his crop, he still keeps his head. He knows that the warm sun will return the following year, and his first thought is always for the new growth.

9

The Myth of the Magic Expense Account

Has expense-account entertaining gone beyond the limits of propriety and good sense? Is there the possibility of a severe political reaction?

WHEN A Japanese businessman is ready to close a big deal, he would not think of doing it in his office. Instead, the seller takes the buyer out to dinner. While the *sukiyaki* simmers slowly toward fragrant perfection over the charcoal brazier in the corner of the quaint little room, they curl their legs comfortably beneath them under the low table. Quietly, they begin to talk. First they inquire solicitously for the welfare of their respective families. Then, cautiously, they approach the subject which is uppermost in their minds. Unobtrusively a *geisha* fills and refills their fragile cups with warm *sake*, and from time to time croons a soft Oriental melody to the accompaniment of her *samisen*. Hours later, they sign.

I doubt that Rudyard Kipling had observed this ceremony when he said that East is East, and West is

West, and that never the twain should meet. I see little difference in principle between what goes on in Tokyo and what goes on in various night spots and resort hotels in the United States when the big expense-account money gets flowing. True, the *samisen* has not yet been widely employed in plush American restaurants, but there are those in our business community who seem to agree fully with their Japanese colleagues that the uninhibited use of high-priced food and liquor will move merchandise.

Certain it is that entertaining by business in this country is now itself big business. Some companies are more widely known for their parties than they are for their products. The occasions for business entertainment range all the way from two for lunch in the executive dining room to several thousand in the ballroom of the big hotel, with name bands, and orchids flown in from Hawaii for the ladies.

Gone are the days when a salesman occasionally wined and dined his favorite customer, or perhaps gave a small theater party. Nowadays, when the deal gets big enough, the company yacht weighs anchor and moves into position, the company plane takes off for a duck blind in Arkansas, or the best hotel in Miami throws open its doors to expectant dealers for a week of continuous circus.

The distaff side is cut in, too, on both sides of the

deal. How the ladies love it! With jet travel what it is, those who were getting a little tired of White Sulphur may now hope to look in on Capri or the Riviera.

The unseen partner in all this largesse, of course — the man who rides the afterdeck of the company's yacht, co-pilots the duck hunters' plane, sits by while the caviar is spooned out and the *crêpes suzettes* are sizzling — the man who splits the check at the night spot and hands the big bill to the headwaiter — is none other than Uncle Sam. Lights would go dim along the Strip in Las Vegas and chorus girls would be unemployed from New York to Los Angeles if it were not for that great modern invention, the tax deduction.

But who are the silent underwriters of this frenetic spending? You and I, the general taxpayers. It is we who make up to the United States Treasury the revenue lost through expense-account deductions.

This orgiastic abuse of the expense account is by no means universal, or even in a broad sense characteristic of our business community today. It is, however, a spectacular and alarming trend, participated in by enough companies and individuals to put all of us upon caution for the good reputation of businessmen as a class.

So far, expense-account entertainment is held somewhat in check by two factors.

First of all, the best companies — those who value the good opinion of thoughtful people — reject it. They behave with dignity and self-restraint in relationship with their customers.

Secondly — and this is altogether discreditable — in some of those companies that practice excesses, the president himself has no part in it. He lives correctly in his suburb, stays out of the hot spots. He just passes the word to the general auditor not to bear down. Expense accounts from the operating department get tough treatment — but not those from the sales end of the business. And the dirty work is delegated to the younger men. They catch on fast. They know that the boss prefers not to be told all that goes on.

Just over the horizon a third limitation is coming somewhat hazily into view. It may actually mark the cut-off of all this excess, if the spenders are smart enough to notice it, which I doubt.

That third limitation is rising public indignation. An ordinary fellow — say, an executive from a public utility where every penny is scrubbed before it is spent — takes his wife out to dinner for the one big evening of the year. He finds at the next table a neighbor who has just ordered his third bottle of champagne, although he is known to be two payments behind on his car. And the ordinary, decent citizen doesn't like what he sees. He cannot deduct his wife's dinner from his personal income tax as an expense, and he resents watching someone else live it up for free. So, when they hear about it second hand from waiters and hatcheck girls, do teachers and policemen and others who have just had a pay raise denied. So do I. And so does anyone else who understands and values the free enterprise system.

This may be the next spectacular issue for the politicians if the present ominous grumbling grows into a ground swell. An attack on business is sure fire in many Congressional districts. Nothing goes over better than to expose special privilege which is not available to the ordinary citizen.

When that time comes, the innocent will suffer with the guilty, as they always do, and legitimate promotional and development effort will be restricted or made more costly.

There already have been warnings from the Executive Branch of the government, with concurrences from Capitol Hill, that entertaining as a legitimate business expense will come in for serious restudy.

It is disturbing that business does not put its own house in order while there is still time, that it does not speak out boldly against expense-account abuses.

The whole purpose of a trade association, or of any nationwide industrial organization, is to provide a collective voice on matters of mutual concern. The trouble is that we use that voice steadily against others but seldom turn it inward toward ourselves. We are trigger-happy with criticism of government, but reluctant when it comes to self-criticism. We are quick to point out the excesses of labor — and rightly so — but if we were equally ready to point out our own, they might more speedily be corrected.

That individual business leaders do not publicly denounce such abuses more often, even when they do not practice them themselves, is not surprising, though still regrettable. "Judge not that ye not be judged" applies. Each one of us feels a certain inhibition against appointing himself a critic of others' conduct. Yet this qualm disappears when it is a collective judgment made in concert with colleagues through a national organization. If such bold leadership for the correction of excesses cannot thus be achieved, free enterprise has an extremely vulnerable Achilles heel. If we cannot correct these things ourselves, we can hardly protest if government steps in to do it for us.

But beyond these moral overtones, and the damage currently being done to the good name of business in the eyes of the general public, comes a practical question. Do these practices, in fact, pay off? There would seem to be serious reason to doubt whether lavish display and heavy-handed entertaining are really worth the cost, whether in the long run they actually sell the merchandise.

Those who indulge in such methods are notoriously poor judges of people. They seem to think that God made all men in their image. The salesman who resorts to the nightclub approach is usually a man who likes nightclubs. It never occurs to him that the man on the other side of the transaction might just possibly prefer to stay home, have a quiet evening with his family, and go to bed early.

Or take race tracks. Oddly enough, there are some people who would rather potter around with roses in a garden than go out and bet on the horses. Quite often they are the very ones who get asked to go to the Derby in a private car.

In the earlier days of the automotive industry, the favorite technique was for a salesman to go to Detroit, organize an all-night poker game, and lose heavily to the chief purchasing agent. This approach lost sight of the fact that there are strange characters who would rather read a book in front of a fire than play deuces wild and absorb bourbon until dawn.

What a man does with his time after hours is purely personal, and more often than not it is sharply divorced from his business. Selling that forgets this is not shrewd.

In other words, on the law of chances, there are probably as many men who will be offended, even insulted, by over-expenditure to win their favors as there are those who will be impressed.

Sometimes the use of entertainment and gifts reaches the point where it crosses the line of proper customer relationships altogether and becomes commercial bribery. A set of golf clubs at Christmas to the third assistant purchasing agent, or a carton of cigarettes with a hundred-dollar bill tucked inside, is completely venal. Business purchased by such means has too precarious a base to be enduring. Yet, strangely enough, some companies that would fire instantly any employee who accepted such gifts from others nevertheless permit their own salesmen to make them. Surely, maintaining such a dual standard is less than honest.

The really fine salesman never mistakes his mission. For example, he never yields to the temptation of selling himself instead of his merchandise. He has but one thing to offer, and that is the product of his company. He submerges his own personality in the composite structure of the company team, so that there will be no break in continuity should circumstances cause him to be replaced.

114

His highest function is to determine with precision the customers' needs, even when they are not clearly understood by the buyer — as they often are not — and to make sure that his company can serve those requirements adequately. His knowledge of wines and his skill at cards are better employed when made available to his friends than when they are substituted for knowledge of his own business and that of the customer.

In the long run, the product must sell itself. It takes on no added value from exposure to neon lights, nor is it likely that its special virtues can be explained more clearly at two in the morning than at two in the afternoon. If it is insufficient in quality or uncertain in delivery, no amount of entertaining can long conceal those basic deficiencies. You can cover up a crack in the wall temporarily with whitewash, but the defect will keep coming back indefinitely until the wall is repaired.

The only relationship between seller and buyer that will endure through the years is one which rests solidly upon mutual satisfaction and understanding. No such lasting commercial partnership can be purchased with champagne. Nor can it be induced by a shallow effusion of insincere friendship from a show-off who has been given a fat expense account. Purchasers who bear substantial responsibility are intelligent and serious-minded executives. They want to deal with selling officers who are also intelligent and thoughtful, and who behave in a responsible manner. They have little respect for playboys.

Objective students of the current business scene must view this phenomenon of the reckless use of expense-account money with considerable dismay. They would be hard to convince that extravagant parties make a significant contribution to the nation. Party or no party, the commodity to be sold remains the same, having no greater utility for the buyer afterwards than before, and no greater profit potential for the seller. To say these things, however, is something of a waste of breath — for those on the lunatic fringe of industry who commit the excesses are not given to taking serious thought for the welfare of the economy or for the preservation of the private enterprise system in the midst of the great world struggle in which we are engaged.

They seldom pause to speculate on what image of the American free economy their conduct creates in the minds of men from the new countries who come to study our way of life. From Pakistan to Nigeria, from Ecuador to Indonesia, the battle is on between socialism and free enterprise. Which will be the basis for developing untapped industrial strength? We are the models upon whom men who wish to preserve private initiative in their economies base their hopes.

We cannot be too careful in what we teach them. They imitate the bad as readily as they do the good, and they may easily attribute our success to the wrong causes.

Selling is a high test of character, perhaps more so than production itself. Much of it takes place away from the watchful eye of prudent supervision. The individual is on his own, and his conduct will rise no higher than his own capacity to do right because it *is* right, when no one in authority is at hand to check him. Those who select and train him must have this in mind. They must not be deceived by suave manners and a ready gift of speech.

Above all, the right tone must be set at the top.

10

The Myth of the Overworked Executive

*Pity the overworked executive! Behind his
paperwork ramparts, he struggles bravely
with a seemingly superhuman load of
responsibilities. Burdened with impossible
assignments, beset by constant emergencies,
he never has a chance to get organized.
Pity him — but recognize him for
the dangerous liability he is.*

A FINE automobile is one of the miracles of modern engineering. Beneath the hood lies unlimited power, ready to lunge into immediate action at the slightest touch of the accelerator. Yet there is no unseemly outward manifestation of that power. Stand beside the car when the engine is running and you scarcely hear a sound. There is no observable movement or vibration.

You cannot see the brakes, but they are wondrously efficient. The power can easily be released, but it can instantly be brought back under control. The car is always on the alert, always ready to do its job, but it is constructed for easy guidance and complete control at all times.

We have fine business executives who are like that. Their behavior is marked by outward calm and poise.

Underneath lies tremendous personal capacity and power. Great effort is not signaled by outward commotion. They can take decisive action without breaking through the barriers of orderly restraint. In the African jungle, the lion roars as he springs for the kill, but among executives, those who are the leaders can exert their greatest strength without lifting their voices.

I am not, however, writing of these men, but of their opposites.

In nearly every organization there is a self-appointed overworked executive. All day, every day, he advertises his martyrdom. His, he believes, is the pivotal responsibility in his company. Constantly sorry for himself because of the enormous burden he bears, he calls all men to witness the sacrifices he makes for the good of the company, sacrifices so little appreciated by his superior officers. Privately, and yet to all who will listen, he pours out his personal woe, which is that he is badly underpaid.

Here is how you will know him: His desk is a mess. Papers are strewn across it in wild disarray, creating the impression that every important corporate transaction comes to him for approval. Yet if you should discreetly make a few spot-checks, you would find that many of the letters and memos which he paws through to find the one you are after were there last week. They will be there next week, too. Should you find one day, to your surprise, a slight improvement, you would probably later discover that he achieved this in desperation by sweeping an armful of papers into the desk drawer.

Close by our hero's elbow is a large ash tray, half full of partly smoked cigarettes, to indicate the extreme nervous tension under which he operates.

He seldom goes out to lunch, but has a sandwich and a glass of milk brought in. This adds to the build-up. Not a moment of his time must be lost, or earnings for the month will go off sharply.

In his hand when he leaves the office is the inevitable bulging briefcase. He would no more be caught without that mark of martyrdom than he would be seen without his trousers. True, many of the papers in it have already made a great many round trips without being disturbed. But nevertheless this nightly show makes it clear to all that here is a very important man.

When finally he bursts in the front door of his house, he pecks his wife hastily on the cheek and expects to sit down at the table immediately. He must never be kept waiting. He has dropped his briefcase in the front hall, where it is likely to stay till morning if there should happen to be a night ball game on. At best it will be a tug-of-war between the papers and the blare of television for several hours. There will be little general family conversation.

One of this man's proudest boasts is that he has not had a vacation in ten years. "Just can't take the time," he says. That his wife deserves one, and that his family is growing up without the joy of experiences shared with him, are considerations outside his realm of understanding. Actually, his capacity for enjoyment is so atrophied that he would not know what to do with a vacation if forced into it. Nonetheless he will soon have one involuntarily — in a hospital — when his coronary thrombosis comes, as it surely will.

He is greatly given to travel, rushing about on planes, briefcase in hand, as though the number of miles flown in a year were any criterion of effective effort. Physical activity gives him a proud sense of doing. Often a long-distance call, if prudently planned and intelligently carried through, would fully answer the purpose; but that would somehow downgrade the whole transaction. Nor does he ever achieve much by correspondence, since he has never learned to express himself cogently and persuasively in a letter.

What little responsibility he bears he shares with no one. To simplify his day by delegating to juniors the routine clerical part of his tasks would deflate his ego. Neither superior officer nor associate is ever quite sure just what it is that occupies him so intensively. If something takes him away from his desk, whether for an hour or for a week, everything stops.

Partly this is because it gives him satisfaction to surround himself with a slight air of mystery. For example, he is highly secretive about his personal affairs. He would not think of letting a secretary handle his checkbook or take his deposits to the bank. She might find out how small his income really is in comparison with the image he is endeavoring to create.

He has never had a will drawn, has never had a frank talk with his wife as to what to do or whom to consult in case of his death, or told her what she may expect by way of income during her remaining years. His meager insurance policies are not collected in one place, and his social security card is long since lost.

He is chronically late for all engagements. When a staff conference is called, he bustles into the room fifteen minutes after it has been begun, wearing an air of preoccupation which is intended to suggest to his colleagues that it is generous indeed for a man who bears such manifest responsibility to take time for such lesser matters at all.

In his office he keeps visitors waiting beyond the time set for the engagement, partly because his awareness of his surroundings is so low that he is actually not conscious of the passage of time, and partly because by delaying others he reminds himself once more of his own importance.

The presence of such a disordered life within an organization can have repercussions that are the very antithesis of good management. Inevitably, this man becomes a focal point from which confusion and uncertainty spread. Policy is neither reliably implemented by such an individual nor accurately transmitted to others. Because he cannot discipline himself, he can neither lead nor discipline others.

The fault lies within. What is missing is the inner poise and deep humility that comes from the continuous development of the adult mind and spirit.

A person of this type is almost invariably one who early abandoned the cultivation of the mind. Yet, sadly enough, he is more often than not a college graduate. He has no intellectual satisfactions. From one year's end to the next he never enters into the companionship of great minds by good reading. He confines himself strictly to the daily paper, principally the financial and sporting sections, and to his trade journals. He hears no concerts, attends no art exhibits, participates in no discussion groups. He has no views on the questions of the day other than a continuing stream of verbose invective directed toward all those in authority.

In the realm of the spirit, he possesses no basic

philosophy to which he may turn in times of stress. He has no sense of values that find expression in his life from day to day, values which others come to recognize and respect.

Yet mental serenity and internal resources are never lacking in the truly great executives of American industry. They must, of course, have fine minds and strong wills. But the power of their personalities finds expression through order and a self-discipline so immaculate that it is seldom apparent as a separable trait of character.

When a visitor is shown in to a good executive, he finds before him a clean desk and behind it a man who is at ease, who makes him feel that this is the call he has been waiting for, and who listens attentively. Yet, subtly, the man behind the desk is in control of the interview all of the time and knows how to terminate it without giving offense.

The good executive also has a plan for his day. He knows what things have to be accomplished if the required tempo is to be maintained, and times himself accordingly. With deliberate speed he moves from one task to the next, making his decisions resolutely when he senses the matter has consumed the maximum period that can be allotted to it. There is no outward sign of inner struggle, and the job gets done.

He works a full day, though not an overly long one.

127

When the normal quitting time comes, except for those sudden emergencies which no man can control, he will walk promptly out of his office with a sense of satisfaction at what he has accomplished. And in closing the door, he will put it all behind him. His evenings and his weekends bring him a change of pace. In company with his family and neighbors, he turns with high enthusiasm to other challenging interests that are totally unrelated to his daily routines. When he comes back to his job, both his body and his mind have been refreshed.

His ideas do not become inbred, because he spends a great deal of time with people who know nothing whatever about his business and who are not particularly impressed with his responsibilities. Many of them do not even know what he does, and care less. This helps him keep his own importance in perspective.

He has a zest for vacations. He knows that rotation of interest is as important to the productivity of the mind as rotation of crops is to the fertility of the soil.

He has the excellent characteristic of laughing well. His lively and infectious sense of humor lubricates all of his human relationships.

In short, the self-pitying, overworked executive is a man who presses badly. The fine executive is one who always takes a free, easy swing at the ball.

11

The Myth of the
Wicked Politician

*Despite the current enthusiasm about "getting
into politics," in the back of his mind many a
businessman sees government as a nest of wily
politicos and bumbling bureaucrats who
couldn't honestly make a go of it
in business if they tried.*

FOR MANY American businessmen, "politics" is a dirty word.

And, strangely enough, for many politicians, "business" is a dirty word.

Both are wrong, and something should be done about it. The businessman needs the skills of the politician, and the politician needs the skills of the businessman. Neither can afford to call the other bad names. It is not true that all politicians lack principle, and not true that the businessman responds only to self-interest. Dishonesty and selfishness are human defects that are attributes of a particular human being, not symbols of a calling. It would be my guess that they are found in about equal proportions among both politicians and businessmen.

Let us pause to consider what the admirable qualities are in the politician, and then ask ourselves whether those qualities have value for the businessman.

First comes tough-mindedness. The politician knows what he wants and goes after it with vigor and tireless perseverance. He goes round, through, or over every obstacle and never quits so long as there remains a single chance of getting there.

Next comes flexibility. It is the goal that the politician keeps in mind. He is willing to change the method as often as he thinks it is necessary to improve his chance to advance. He is not rigid about nonessentials. He will take the half loaf if the full package of bread just isn't there. On the battlefield, he will not commit suicide for glory if the strategic retreat will bring him the ultimate victory.

He has a warm human interest in people. There is no person in any walk of life whose opinion he does not value. He listens. This is not the studied pose of an actor but an instinct, and if he did not have it, he would not be a politician. He has a sensitive awareness of all that goes on about him and is constantly readjusting his judgments of people and events in the light of new evidence or changed conditions.

The politician is, of course, articulate. He communicates constantly and has the knack of saying things that people remember. He is at his very best when saying no, for his negative is almost as pleasant as his affirmative.

His memory is fantastic, but this is merely a result of the sharpness of his power of observation. He pays close attention to all that others say and gets a clear image of what he sees. Awareness again.

He has loyalty. He never breaks his word, and he helps those who help him. Moreover, he is never too proud to accept help.

Of course, the successful politician has many other fine qualities too — including honor, which is basic in all walks of life — and all of them would seem to be equally desirable for the businessman. It has been wisely said that no man can become a statesman unless he is first a politician — meaning that he must first get elected. With equal justice it might be said that few businessmen get to the top who do not manifest in their conduct the same qualities we attribute to politicians.

Take tough-mindedness, for example. Business is not a debating society; it is a field of action. The executive who does not know precisely what he is trying to accomplish will fail, for he will transmit his uncertainty to all those about him, and group ineffectiveness will be inevitable. There are two principal reasons why the vacillating executive lacks the quality of tough-mindedness: Either he does not possess the intellectual acumen to analyze a problem clearly and formulate a plan decisively, or he lacks the moral courage to put it through. When he swerves, everyone around him swerves, and soon the whole affair is in a muddle. Just as a saddle horse knows instinctively when the rider is afraid, so the morale of an entire department in any company can sink to the vanishing point if the boys sense with dismay that the boss either doesn't know or doesn't dare. Leadership is contagious singleness of purpose, radiant confidence of success for a clearly defined program, and tough-mindedness is the base.

But tough-mindedness without flexibility is the stubbornness born of ignorance. Some men with really great purposes and fine ideas stalk through their business careers meeting frustration at every turn because they lack change of pace. They seem determined that if it is not to be done their way, it shall not be done at all. Deep inside a frigid exterior lies tragic insecurity. The truly confident man, he who bases his assurance on genuine humility, senses no weakness in a change of plan, so long as he still advances toward his goal. Nor does he fear to abandon the goal entirely if with earnest open-mindedness he examines the thinking of his associates and finds reasonable doubt as to its wisdom. Sheer bullheadedness, which is often mistaken for courage, builds no successful plants and sells no products.

It is not surprising that many businessmen who call for more skillful diplomacy in the conduct of our foreign affairs practice so little of it themselves, for diplomacy is fairly rare in human nature and not easily defined. Yet we all know what we are talking about when we say privately that the boss "just hasn't got it."

One wonders, too, to what extent lack of talent for compromise is responsible for the sad deadlocks that occur in collective bargaining between management and labor. These deadlocks often go on solely because a negotiator seizes the chance to display his ego. Usually, we appoint lawyers or economists as mediators. Perhaps we should designate politicians instead. They might find a way out when no one else can. At least, they would lubricate the frictions with common sense and be alert for compromise with honor.

As to the sensitivity toward human values which the politician displays, we simply cannot live without it in business. Not only for the good of the company but for our own peace of mind, we simply must make a go of it with the man who works alongside us. We do this by building our relationships on each other's good points and not letting the other man's limitations close our eyes to his strong qualities.

Some men never succeed in making such adjustments. They either live in a constant state of guerilla warfare with those about them or clam-up in silent and morose isolation. Such an individual is a cancerous growth within an otherwise normal organization and must be removed as soon as discovered, no matter how painful the surgery. Quite often he has a brilliant mind, and there are many spots, such as research, where he may work alone and contribute much. But he is out of place where teamwork is involved.

As to the quality of being articulate, which all top politicians possess and which many businessmen lack, I am not clear whether a man becomes a politician because he possesses it or whether he acquires it because it is indispensable to his calling. Whichever hypothesis is correct, I can only wish that all executives had it too. No man can exercise vigorous leadership who does not have the gift of transmitting thought, both by the spoken and the written word. No plan is valid, no program significant, if the man who conceives it is unable to communicate it to others, and this is a function which he cannot delegate.

Memory, as such, is an attribute to which I give a low rating. I am always suspicious of the man who can infallibly quote statistics, and who takes pride in correcting others on dates and other trivia. The important thing about data is to know where to find them when you need them. It's not necessary to make a filing cabinet out of your brain. The highest function of the mind is the exercise of judgment, and there is no correlation between a capacity to reason and factual memory. But sensitivity to one's surroundings and awareness of the impact upon our own thought and action of that which occurs around us is of top priority.

Loyalty in business is simple honesty. To hold fast to friendship, whether in business or in politics, is an elementary expression of high character. It would be highly worthwhile even if it were not good business, which it always is. Only those unfortunate men who have no scale of moral values to which they hold fast reject it.

Then there are two other characteristics which are not the special property of either politicians or businessmen but which, when practiced by either group, greatly enhance the effectiveness of politics in its best meaning.

The first is a lively sense of humor — not heavy-handed buffoonery, or coarseness, or ill-timed satire that hurts, but a deft instinct for the infectious chuckle. How many times in daily business life there comes a tense moment, a situation when tempers are running high and irreparable damage might be done by an angry outburst, that a wise man with ready wit saves by a spontaneous flash of humor! Most effective of all is the man who dares to laugh at himself, for no one can fight him when that is his posture.

Finally comes the heaven-sent instinct which some men have for performing little acts of personal consideration and kindness for those about them without thought of recompense of any sort. This may be as simple as remembering that a man's child is ill and asking for it correctly by name, or as important as offering an unsolicited loan that you know is desperately needed. It is the spirit of the thing that counts, for the intangible values that mean so much in sound human relations, whether in public life or in the shop or the office, lie chiefly in the realm of the spirit. They cannot be learned by rote or bought with money.

Why, then, if businessmen possess these fine qualities in equal measure with politicians, and if the exercise of these personal attributes brings equally profitable results to both, should they regard each other with suspicion? Would it not be better if they learned to pool their abilities and to work toward a strong economy and a better government?

More specifically, why doesn't the businessman overcome his distaste for "dirty politics" and throw himself into the political arena and personally work to correct the abuses of which he complains? Revolutionary as this about-face would be, it would electrify the country.

One simple, vital change is all that is needed: the creation of a new climate for political activity within business organizations. Let the men at the top set a new tone, so that seeking and holding public office is honorable instead of dangerous for individual employees, and the revolution is on.

It is too late for the men of my generation to take the plunge themselves. They are frozen in by their inhibitions, but the young men are ready. Those between twenty-five and forty-five years of age, sobered by war and alarmed at the uncertainties that lie ahead for their children, are champing at the bit. All that they ask is to be turned loose and given their heads.

This is radical, but it will work. It will certainly help to clean up politics, if top management will go all out. They must make it absolutely clear that freedom to participate in political activity, on company time when proper, extends to every level of the company and applies impartially to members of both parties. Let the assistant safety engineer in the plant be just as free to serve as township road supervisor as the vice president is to be a member of the board of education. And let Republican officers honestly encourage effort by Democratic precinct workers.

My generation abandoned the political arena to the professionals by default. It can now be recaptured by younger men, if those presently at the management controls will give the go signal.

12

The Myth of the
Perfect Balance Sheet

*The financial statement may reflect a
company's past, but how much does it tell
of the future — or of the men whose actions,
today, determine tomorrow's profits?*

"THE KING was in the countinghouse, counting out his money."

What a field day that must have been for the financial analyst of the time! There the old boy sat, smugly piling up the bullion in neat rows. Incredibly solvent, he owed no man a farthing. The glory of his ancestors shone round about him. Tenaciously he guarded the cash that had been handed down to him — but he was blind to what was going on outside the palace. He did not realize that he was presiding over the disintegration of his kingdom.

We have companies like that — fine old institutions with great names and impressive records, which begin to fall apart long before that sinister fact is recognized by the investing public. They, too, are incredibly solvent, but the strength of the balance sheet is merely a façade that conceals the decay within.

To forecast the future of a company by studying its financial statements only, without intimate knowledge of the personal capacity of those who constitute the management, is like prophesying the weather without knowing which way the kind is blowing. The balance sheet is the record of a corporation's past, not a guide to its future. The best of earnings statements may prove nothing but that the company still has momentum from what has gone before.

Human resources are far more significant for a corporation's future than physical assets, and to assume that because it is rich today it will be richer tomorrow is a *non sequitur*.

For many groups in our country, the future of a particular corporation is of tremendous importance. There is the investor who is trying to keep his capital both gainfully and safely employed, the professional investment analyst who advises others, and the financial commentator who writes for others. But there are also many more: executives who are planning mergers or acquisitions, men who may be considering management positions in a certain company, the annual crop of college graduates who are looking for jobs. Those among them who are wise have learned to give more weight to an informed evaluation of people than to an appraisal of visible values.

It was 1932 when the searing experience came

which imposed the countinghouse mentality on many of the men who today are still in management. They saw bank deposits frozen, receivables defaulted, and general paralysis spread throughout the business community. Cash was all that counted, and they determined never again to let their companies be caught without it. So they put security above daring and have bequeathed to their successors solvent, but moribund, institutions.

The investor should never think of the balance sheet as anything more than one factor, among many, to be weighed. To begin with, it does not always give a true picture even of the past. It shows how much money has been spent, but not necessarily how wisely the capital has been used. It may, and usually does, represent imagination and bold thinking on the part of earlier leadership. Yet it may be merely the mausoleum in which their errors of judgment and their timidity have been interred.

Consider the location of plants, for example. Maybe the small group which first started the business lived in a particular area and understandably wanted to go on making their homes in the place of their birth. Conditions change, however. For a business to go on expanding in the old area through sheer inertia, instead of responding to new forces and recognizing altered circumstances, may be complete folly. Stubbornness is not always wisdom. The brick-and-mortar values as recorded on the books may be correct, but building new additions to old plants may reflect cowardice rather than courage. A critical survey may reveal that newer, competing companies have been building plants in what are now seen to be the right locations, and that they are steadily increasing their share of the total business. Such young companies may have a less desirable ratio of assets to liabilities, yet their life expectancy can be quite superior. When the process goes far enough, the old and rich company suddenly finds with dismay that its liquidating value is all that it has left.

Nor is this weakness limited just to the comparison of locations within the United States.

Crisp and uninhibited reaching-out for new markets is now going forward on a world scale. Old companies that have stayed young, as well as those which — though fragile financially — have recaptured the daring of our ancestors, are now taking the plunge overseas. There lie the great new markets of the future.

It has been our tradition, both individual and corporate, that success often stems from necessity. Complacency is its foe. The plain truth is that the entire economy of the free world is moving inevitably toward total integration, driven by forces which no one country can control or divert, let alone one man or one company. Those who, instead of leaping lustily into the struggle of world competition, continue to sit smugly in the countinghouse, looking comfortably to tariffs and quotas to safeguard their solvency, may suffer slow strangulation.

Yet a changing market pattern which is neither clearly seen nor courageously faced is not the only cause of senescence. Sources of supply change, too, and take a heavy toll in cost, though you might study the annual statement of a dying company indefinitely without discovering that this process had begun to affect its affairs. The finished product of one company is the incoming raw material for the next. If, in the chain of manufacture, one supplier is forced by economic circumstances either to abandon its operations altogether or to change location, all others in the sequence must make suitable adjustments. Whether they do that promptly and effectively depends on people.

The American steel industry, as it developed in the early part of this century, located its plants where it did because it drew iron ore from Minnesota and Michigan, transporting it down the Great Lakes. Now a very substantial part of the required ore must be brought in from such far-off points as Labrador, Sweden, Africa, and Venezuela, and all those earlier decisions have to be re-evaluated.

Nor does the current earnings statement constitute a safe index as to whether the corporation will be a happy ship for the future in terms of the vital personal relationships between executives in the management group. Outward appearances can be very deceptive. Two men who bear the deepest animosity toward each other can be skillful in maintaining the amenities. If, however, the vice-president in charge of operations and the financial officer are sharpening their knives for each other, and the president isn't man enough to knock their heads together, trouble lies ahead. Or if nepotism is rampant, with the boss determined to promote not only his son but his wife's younger brother, dangerous tensions exist which sooner or later will slow the company's progress.

Poor health is a similar hidden menace. If the chief medical officer knows that a key executive is ignoring a high-blood-pressure problem which could take him off the team without warning, and the personnel officer knows that nothing is being done about training his successor, they possess dangerously pertinent information about the company's future.

And where is the financial seismograph that is sensitive enough to forecast the eruption of a major stockholders' row in an old company? The new muscle men who stalk stealthily along the outer reaches of the stock market, ready to pounce on the unwary, seem to prefer rich but somnolent companies, those with a great past but doubtful future. Usually the first warning that comes to the investing public that the kill has been made is when the financial vultures start soaring overhead.

Another significant area where a company's financial statement offers no sure guide to its future is its competence in its own field of technology, when compared with that of its competitors. Research is the lifeblood of industry. Some companies steal new advances in technology, some borrow, some buy; but only those who consistently do their own research are a safe buy for the investor. Growth cannot be superimposed from the outside: It has to come from within, and to develop a superior research staff takes long, patient effort.

In industry, as in all other aspects of human affairs, people are more important than things. Yet in gauging the soundness of a business institution we have no recognized procedures through which an outsider may form his own judgment as to the quality of the management.

We have certified public accountants who examine the books and reassure us that the securities which the company reports it holds actually do exist. We have no certified personnel inspectors who inventory the younger executives available to sustain the company's future, no certified public psychologists to measure the brain power and test the emotional stability of those now exercising leadership.

Often, in a particular corporation, there will be one man — and only one — who is widely known to the general public. Sometimes he and the company are so closely identified, both in his own mind and that of the outsider, that they are practically synonymous. He may be both extrovert and able, or just extrovert. If able, he may carry the whole show himself, giving little opportunity to those below him either to display or to develop talent — in which case his death or disability can bring disaster. On the other hand, if he is only mediocre as to talent, though articulate, he may nevertheless have instinctive insight into his own limitations, and thus delegate responsibility, so that his very weakness permits a strong team to develop.

Quite often the strongest man in a management group, the one who is wisest in counsel and most resourceful in meeting the unexpected, is all but unknown outside the intimate inside circle because of his innate modesty and his studied habit of permitting his talents to find expression through the activities of others.

Certain it is that the annual report will give no help in distinguishing the prudent from the reckless among the officers, or the wise from the merely uninhibited. The names of all will be there, but not a statement as to their respective qualifications. You will find pictures of the new plant, but not of the new vice-president. Nor will you find any explanation of why he had to be hired from the outside instead of promoted from within.

Conceivably, however, the day may come in our surge toward more effective business techniques when a new professional group will come into being. Upon demand, they will perhaps survey objectively the human potential of a management group, and certify it to the public just as an accounting firm certifies the company's financial potential.

When that times comes, what will the practitioners of this new profession inquire into?

Surely they will search the records to determine the organization's reserves of people, just as the accountant searches the records to determine the reserves for plant replacement. They will want to know just who is next in line for each key post, and whether he is competent to assume a higher responsibility.

But an inventory of people in terms of their number in ratio to posts of responsibility would be only the first element in the inquiry. Far more important would be an appraisal of the total capacity of the entire management group in terms of leadership effectiveness.

How would this hypothetical new profession proceed to determine the quality of men? Sheer intellectual capacity could be tested with a fair degree of accuracy, if both the company and the individuals concerned would permit these future auditors of ability to make the same penetrating inquiries into intelligence as financial auditors now make into probity.

Yet by what system of tests could such professionals, no matter how highly trained, measure the vital but abstract quality of leadership?

There is the crux of the whole matter. Leadership — that intangible, hard-to-define something that sets some men apart, that blend of native talent and cultivated attributes, that radiant and inspiring gift that causes some men unerringly to choose the right and to give others faith that it is right — leadership, whether God-given or man-cultivated, holds the key to the future in the business world.

I am led to wonder, therefore, whether we are as far advanced in management methods and practices as we think. We concern ourselves so much with the question of financial solvency, and so little with that of human solvency.

Actually, a good balance sheet is like the foundation for a house. It is important, but nobody lives in it. Everything that counts happens above that level.

13

The Myth of the Slick Purchasing Agent

To salesmen, an ogre — bullying, crafty, and venal. To management, a lackey — indispensable but unrespected, and not always trusted. Such is the purchasing agent of legend, whose image is fast being displaced by the reality of today's trained, responsible purchasing executive.

TIME WAS when purchasing was a shoddy affair. The company buyer was a little man in the back room. He usually worked with his coat off, even in the winter. Inevitably he kept rolling a half-smoked cigar around in his mouth, and he held a short pencil between his fingers. He bought on price, and price only.

He loved to "sweat" the salesman. He would tell each that a competitor had quoted a lower figure, and let the poor anguished soul guess, at his peril, whether or not the buyer was telling the truth, which he usually wasn't. If the commodity was one that was "stabilized" by the big producers and had a firm price that could not be broken, the buyer would sign the contract but take a side agreement that the seller would later accept billing for a fake claim based upon an alleged shortage in quantity or defect in quality. This had the advantage that the supplier could covertly show the signed agreement to his competitor to prove that the price had not been cut.

This buyer's basic technique was to make all callers wait. Deliberate discourtesy seemed to be the only human approach he knew. His stuffy little reception room was often crowded, but he always took his time.

He would not only play one supplier against another, but within the same company whipsaw one man against another, hoping to get a break by catching them off guard. And don't think for a moment that he was above taking a kickback for himself.

In his ignorance he did not realize that he was defeating his own ends. He had the short pencil, but those with whom he dealt had the long memories. Behind the mask of their professional salesman smiles lay eternal loathing. As deception was piled upon deception and insult upon insult, they swore to take their revenge and square accounts. In the fullness of time they always did.

When the wheel of the economy turned round, so that the goods they sold were in short supply and the crafty buyer needed their help badly, they drove in the knife, and drove it deep. It was their turn to make him wait. Even when he was compelled to bid frantically above the market, they found ways to discipline him.

Management paid little attention to all this. Purchasing was then classified as a nonproductive activity. Business was thought to have two important aspects: making a product and selling it. Purchasing was grouped with accounting, research, advertising, and the like, as being on the fringe of utility.

Times suddenly changed with the coming of World War II. Because of the acute procurement difficulties, purchasing was catapulted into prominence. In the transition from a civilian to a war economy, many companies were saved from disaster solely by the ingenuity, persistence, and resourcefulness of their buyers. Highly competent people had to be given the responsibility for this vital function, and they brought new techniques and new standards of conduct.

At the end of hostilities, the sudden surge of demand for consumer goods made it imperative that these new standards be maintained. The atmosphere of the Kasbah was eliminated. The purchasing agent had to be a man of wise judgment and complete honesty of purpose, one who was justly proud of the contribution which he could make to the welfare of his company. Newcomers who now try the old way find to their sorrow that it doesn't pay off.

Yet this vital part of business has not yet created in the minds of young men the image that it is the road to success. In all the years that I personally selected young men from the senior classes of our leading colleges and universities, I do not recall a single occasion when a student, upon being asked what department of the business he thought he would prefer to go into, spoke up eagerly and said "Purchasing."

Every fraternity house has a senior or two of suave manners and supple tongue, making usually only average grades, who can be typed at once for sales. They are sure of it, themselves. Few of the brothers, however, suspect even inwardly that they would make good buyers. Nor can a recruiting officer recognize buyers by any attitude of mind or outward characteristics.

Where then do the fine purchasing men come from? Some men drift into purchasing; others are shoved. The ranks are usually filled by hard-pressed management through sidewise transfers from other activities. Accounting is one source. Oddly enough, the sales department is another, on the hypothesis that a man can be taught to reverse his talents.

Our myopia about purchasing is such that we do not set about the orderly preparation of young men for this career. Pick up the catalogue of any business school. You will find many courses on merchandising, and professors who are nationally known as experts in that field, but seldom will you find the curriculum balanced with equal instruction in purchasing. Yet obviously these activities are reciprocal in significance.

Every commodity that is sold by one company for use in industry is bought by another. The two operations would seem to be of equal dignity and importance.

The same imbalance usually appears also in the development programs within the company itself. In-plant training almost invariably puts more emphasis on selling than it does on buying. Sales trainees are sent through the entire operating sequence, department by department, to become saturated with knowledge of products and processes. Buying juniors spend long hours in the stockroom, see that part of the plant that lies between them and the cafeteria, and learn their part of the business by ear. At the top there might be several vice-presidents in the sales department. Buying is lucky to get one. Presidents seldom come up through purchasing.

Nevertheless, purchasing has arrived, and all this will change. The new philosophy of well-managed companies is that if continuing goodwill and intelligent cooperation is important at the outgoing end of the business between the seller and the customer, then the same sort of relationship should be established between the buyer and the supplier. If service and mutual understanding are important when the company ships to a valued account, it follows that they must be equally effective when acquiring the necessary inbound materials and equipment.

This does not mean, of course, that price is the slightest bit less important. Quite the contrary. Low cost is the lifeblood of the particular company, as it is of the whole American economy, and no part of the company's overall effort is more directly concerned with profit than purchasing.

For many companies a savings of 4 per cent on purchases is equivalent in terms of net profit to a 20 per cent increase in sales. Putting it another way, one could say that every five-dollar reduction in purchasing costs is equal to two dollars and forty cents of increased profit after taxes. This is highlighted by a recent study which showed that to produce one dollar of net profit, sales had to go up nineteen dollars and seventy cents.

But this does not mean that price is everything. That is where the old-time slick purchasing agent with the sharp pencil went wrong.

First of all, low price is often merely a function of low quality. The competent buyer understands this. He has sufficient familiarity with the skills and equipment found in the plant of his supplier, and the requirements of his own, to recognize those situations in which quality must take precedence over price.

The same is true of delivery, service, and performance. He must have the insight to make, and the courage to defend, a decision to the effect that the obligation to perform is beyond the capacity of the offering organization to fulfill. Much better to accept a costlier proposal than to risk everything on the unproven capacity of a shaky new supplier who is trying to break into the field. A lawsuit for damages or a claim against the bonding company is a poor substitute for reliable, on-time delivery and smooth performance.

In making his choice among prospective suppliers, the competent buyer must at all costs assure himself there has been honest and vigorous competition in the bidding. No apparent price advantage can offset the long-term damage that will be done by allowing himself to become known in the trade as an easy mark.

Unhappily, industry has not yet fully put its house in order on this point. In full defiance of both law and morality, purchasing agents are still occasionally framed by salesmen. Suppliers still yield to temptation and shake dice among themselves for jobs. When this happens, the buyer has no alternative but to break up the unconscionable practice by immediate and fearless action, even if the project at hand suffers a serious setback. He should stop at nothing, not even if he invites Federal prosecution that will bring stiff prison sentences.

The ultimate objective of sound purchasing is to build continuing relationships with responsible organizations, and to that end the buyer cultivates his supplier as sedulously as the salesman cultivates his customer. He visits the plant of the other company and learns all he can about its processes. Just as the fine salesman studies the needs of his customer and points out ways in which the latter may improve his costs by changing the specification for the product, so the enlightened buyer points out to his supplier changes in equipment or techniques through which the product or the service which he offers could be bettered.

In building for the future, however, he must develop enough alternative sources of supply to assure a broad base for his company's requirements. His own plant may experience a sudden increase in demand or that of a supplier a sudden loss in capacity. It is his responsibility to hedge both of those risks.

In the building of a strong and enduring relationship there must be give and take. If the discredited habit of frightening and coercing salesmen by cracking a bullwhip over their heads is to be abandoned, it must be replaced by the concept of mutual understanding and joint effort.

The buyer must occasionally tailor his program to suit the exigencies of the other company. By not insisting strictly upon the delivery schedule which would be the absolute best from his point of view, he may be able to relieve a temporary situation that is creating difficulty for his supplier. By giving the supplier as much advance notice as possible when there is to be a change in specifications, or by recognizing a moral obligation toward a company that has made a substantial capital investment for the sole purpose of serving him better, he banks good will for the future.

A special problem is created when the buyer's own company produces a part of its requirements in a particular commodity, and purchases the remainder on the outside. Comes a recession, there is always a strong temptation for the purchasing agent to yield to pressure from his own colleagues and cut the outsiders off cold in order to save the production for the operations of his own people.

Nothing is more damaging to good will or more harmful to the American economy as a whole. When widely indulged in, this practice accentuates the cyclical downswing and distributes the burden unevenly among different groups of workers and varying sections of the country. Carried far enough in an important industry by enough companies, it focuses the hardship in limited areas and calls forth the wasteful processes of government expenditure for aid to distressed communities.

At the national level, this process of putting immediate profit above the welfare of the country can create the most serious complications in our international relationships. For the most part, the new nations around the world have little trade except the export of raw materials. When boom conditions prevail with us, we augment our own dwindling supplies by buying from them. If, when the business cycle turns downward, we at once cut them off, we create disaster for their fragile economies. The Communists know this: they move in as we pull out.

To meet their vastly increased responsibilities, purchasing departments have moved swiftly into the field of data analysis. Good companies, following the example of their sales departments, have added purchasing research as a staff function.

Here keen minds are asking such questions as: Is it necessary? Can a less costly material be used? Are there enough suppliers? Has the supplier sufficient capacity? How much inventory is required in the light of the existing availability and consumption pattern? Is the supplier financially responsible? Are we sufficiently standardized? Are we grouping plant-wide needs for maximum economy?

From such studies, new ideas are emerging and new techniques are being put to use. In fact, few areas of business activity are today in greater ferment with new approaches to industrial problems than is buying. Best of all, top management is now fully alerted to the importance of the receiving end of the business, and fully challenged by the urgency of supporting its efforts.

No longer is the checking of invoices delegated to the office manager. No longer is the decision of what, where, or when to buy made by the owner himself. No longer does the engineer on the job place an order without consulting the man who will be responsible for the operation of the new equipment. Management procedures of the highest standards have replaced the catch-as-catch-can methods of the agent with the drooping cigar and the short pencil. Order is coming out of the chaos.

They are a proud lot, these modern purchasing officers. Their jobs have dignity, and their salaries are commensurate with their new status.

Occasionally, believe it or not, they even take salesmen out to lunch!

14

The Myth of the Rugged Individualist

Have Americans gone soft searching for security? Or have our broad social benefit programs brought compensating advantages to the nation without weakening the individual worker?

THOUGHTFUL AMERICANS everywhere are asking themselves searching questions about what lies ahead for our nation in a world where suddenly we are confronted with a totally alien way of life which seems to be making unmistakable progress.

It is high time, indeed, that we paused to take stock and to make up our minds what are the supreme values and the menacing weaknesses of the American way of life.

Businessmen, particularly, want to know what makes our economy tick, so that they may judge whether we can successfully face up to the new world competition and whether the United States will still be the land of opportunity for their sons and grandsons.

Some say that we are invincible; that the strength

of our system of production, sustained as it is by the creative force of individual initiative, will forge ahead irresistibly, no matter what happens elsewhere.

Others say that we have gone soft; that the clipper-ship daring of our trading ancestors and the fearlessness of the pioneers who conquered the West have been drained from us by the sophistication of modern life; that in the search for security we have lost incentive.

This I challenge. This charge, tragic if true, is in my opinion definitely a myth.

On the contrary, I believe that the modern forms of personal security which now shape our entire society are desirable, in that they give new balance to the economy and bring to the individual a new steadiness of purpose which greatly increases effort.

Certainly the record supports this view and belies the allegation that we have gone soft. The broadening of social benefits has coincided with the greatest surge of industrial expansion that our country has ever known and with the period of our economy's most imaginative and creative resiliency. If these new measures were all evil, we ought to be in a complete tailspin right now.

All of this revolutionary social change has come about in my day. Step by step, I have seen it come to pass — workmen's compensation, unemployment compensation, social security, old age benefits, company pensions, group insurance, special privileges and payments for veterans, health insurance, supplementary unemployment benefits, insured education plans, and all the rest of our complex fabric of social protection for the individual.

I grew up and entered business under the old way, then came to retirement under the new. Almost without exception, I resisted each new change. Almost invariably I was wrong, as it turned out.

We often see the most frightening estimates of what all this costs in terms of percentage of total payroll. Trade association officers, commentators, and professional economists are all prone to ring this particular alarm bell, saying that the cost of fringe benefits has doubled in twelve years. They are fond of computing for various industries what the total social cost amounts to in cents-per-hour of total wage.

This, too, is good. The American people ought to know the precise facts. They should understand clearly what is happening, in order that each citizen may make his own decision as to whether this changing social pattern is good for our country.

But the question is not merely what it costs, but rather what society receives in exchange. Industry has long since learned this lesson from its capital investments for machinery and equipment. It knows that no cost is too high if the value returned is still greater.

Of course, there is a limit to the burden industry can bear, but the trouble here is that the money cost is easily ascertained, while the values received are such that they cannot be charted or tallied on the balance sheet. They must be sensed rather than audited. Only a subtle and willing mind can comprehend them.

What are these values?

Above all, the power that flows from pride of performance, that deep inner satisfaction with life which only a man free from anxiety can experience. No worker comes on the job alone. Inevitably, he carries with him in his thoughts affection for his family and devotion to all the plans and purposes which give meaning to his life. Effort is response to the desire to achieve cherished objectives. Threaten those ideals, suggest that those purposes may be frustrated because of economic insecurity, and reduction of effort inevitably follows. But give him an abiding sense of continuity as he looks toward the future, and certainty of fair play from his employer in the sharing of mutual adversity, and you bring into play one of the strongest motivating forces in human character — loyalty.

In other words, the matter is not so simple as a problem in mathematics, or even in economics. It is also a problem of human relations and of team play in an enlightened democratic society.

It is said, however — rather sententiously — that this broadening pattern of social benefits reduces personal mobility. Factually, the statement is true. But must we assume that this cutting-down of mobility is necessarily bad, from the viewpoint of society as a whole?

At somewhere around the age of thirty-five, the pull of pensions, seniority, and vested interest in the job begins to influence a man, whether he operates a crane or serves as a junior executive, and as the years pass, this pull stiffens until the man is permanently frozen in his job.

Below thirty-five, however, there is still almost complete fluidity. Try to recruit an outstanding member of the senior class of any college, and you will find out quickly how little interest he has in job security or pension plans. All he wants to know is how high the starting salary is and how soon he can get to be a vice president.

There is no substitute for trial and error in arriving at a wise choice with respect to a decision on a lifetime career. A good hunting dog must quarter the field before he can flush the bird.

But there comes a time when, both for his own good and that of the economy, a young man should settle down and square away on a job in which he will get progressively more effective as the years pass. Skill is the product of ability, plus experience. Mastery of a task requires long familiarity, and it seems clear that whatever tends to bring stability into the employment of mature people raises the productivity of all effort and, thus, benefits the economy.

In my earlier years, I lived and worked under the other system, where hiring and firing were daily occurrences and where employment was in a constant state of change. If the man didn't like something the boss said, he laid down his tools and walked off the job. Or conversely, if the man was five minutes late, he was sacked. There was no climate of continuity, no thrifty conservation of experience.

Job jumping of that sort bred industrial vagrancy and was the complete antithesis of orderly promotion. Maximum efficiency and low cost are a result of disciplined team play. The pros will beat the amateurs every time. Furthermore, the instability in character which is either induced by, or reflected in, frequent change of employment will usually find further outlet in domestic unhappiness. All this is neatly glossed over by the use of the phrase "mobility of personnel."

Next, economic writers who are committed to the "mobility" theory say that the heavy cost of providing unemployment benefits causes the employer to pay overtime at premium rates rather than hire additional workers for what may be a short time.

The obvious answer to this is "So what?" The employer gets his added cost back through the greater proficiency of the experienced employees, as compared with green hands, while at the same time he strengthens the important ties of loyalty with the permanent staff. Let it not be forgotten that those who get the overtime pay are the same ones who must take broken time when the sales curve goes down. We may be very sure that the employer will add steadily to his force as soon as he believes that the business has advanced rather permanently to a new plateau, but while it is still dipping up and down, it seems best for all concerned for him to share the "up" with those who must take the "down."

It is said, too, that we have gone so soft in our search for security, have become so accustomed to having others look after us, that we have lost that tough instinct for self-preservation through old-fashioned thrift and far-sightedness which gave fiber to earlier generations of Americans.

This is easier to say than to prove. I, for one, should like to see this frequently recurring statement either documented or dropped, for I read the evidence the other way: I see no letdown today in thrift, no cutoff in the desire to make the future brighter by present sacrifice. In fact, I suspect that the new emphasis on group protection has been educational in effect and has both stimulated and implemented the incentives of personal thrift.

Take housing, for example. Around the great cities in general and industrial plants in particular, new subdivisions are blossoming in bewildering profusion. To own their own home and to have their own bit of good earth upon which the sun and the rain may fall is the ruling passion of every young family today. Twenty-six billion dollars of FHA-insured mortgages now in effect are proof of this.

Or take the purchase of common stocks in industrial companies by employees. Most great corporations now have more stockholders than workers, which was unheard of in the days of complete "mobility" and no social benefits.

No, we have not gone soft. We have just grown more intelligent.

For final proof, ask the Russians. They have stolen generously from capitalism in developing their system of incentives at every step in the process. No businessman with his eyes open can longer doubt that the Russians are realistic or that they are formidable economic competitors. But look closely at what they do, as have many of our industrial teams which have visited their factories, and you will find that they have not only copied our social benefits but have extended them. They are not given to coddling anyone, and their group benefits have not made their workers soft.

So let's stop wringing our hands over the disappearance of "the good old days," when men were rugged individualists and wives were in perpetual panic, and accept the happy fact that the two forces of security and incentive can operate in parallel in our society and contribute jointly to the soundness of our economy.

15

The Myth of the Communist Superman

No businessman succeeds in competition without
the self-confidence that comes from knowing
his own strong points, his rivals'
weaknesses. Yet many of us, alert to the
Soviet trend, are foolishly afraid of learning
the truth about the Communist system.

How LITTLE we American businessmen really know about Communism!

We damn it and we fear it — but we consistently refuse to study it.

In fact, there was a time, and it was not so very long ago, when if a young man had been caught reading Karl Marx he would have been fired out of hand. Even if it had been the boss himself, a whispering campaign would have started that would eventually have compelled him to resign from his club.

I have seen this strange phenomenon go full cycle. As a junior at Harvard in 1911, I was assigned *Das Kapital* as a subject upon which to write a paper. I remember it well, for I entitled my report "Marx and Remarks," a wisecrack which my instructor later told me was responsible for my getting an A minus instead of a B plus in the course. At that time I thought no more of studying Marx than I did of reading De Tocqueville — and I still wish that we could occasionally laugh about Communism instead of always getting so lathered up over it.

Twenty years later, when I was president of a school board, I was severely criticized for opposing the removal of *Das Kapital* from the school library.

And people still point the finger of scorn at me because during the dark days of the last war I made a speech on behalf of Russian War Relief, in which I said that blood shed in front of Stalingrad in the struggle against Hitler was blood shed for me in Chicago.

Even today, when voices are calming down a bit as we adjust to the Communist challenge, I can think of no American businessman who will admit that he has studied either the philosophy or the practices of Communism.

This is not like us, and I do not quite understand it. In the day-to-day operations of our companies, we invariably keep our eyes on the competition. We get hold of copies of the other fellow's catalogue and read it eagerly, page by page. As soon as his new model comes out, we rush one over to the shop so that the boys can take it apart and make a full report. We hire pollsters to find out whether our rival is getting across to the public better than we are. And it would be strange conduct indeed if we should fire a salesman because he asked a dealer what he thought of the other company's merchandise.

We don't behave that way in the field of politics, or religion either. It is still safe — in most places — for a Republican to have lunch with a Democrat, and a Christian minister or priest may study Buddhism or read the Koran without being charged with sacrilege.

But the practitioner of free enterprise who sets out to form his own opinion as to what chance Communism has to supplant our way of life — by examining its tenets and observing its programs — runs great risk of being branded as a subversive.

This attitude is unhealthy. It is cowardice, not strength. It is the abandonment of our tradition of free inquiry. It is the true un-Americanism.

When Khrushchev says he will bury us, we should not get angry. We should gird up our loins and join battle with a cheer, with the banners flying and our breastplates burnished brightly. And not the battle of missiles only — the battle for men's minds the world around as well. We badly need lusty new champions in dialectics — men who love a fight, men who can take Communism apart ideologically and expose it for the social madness that it is, men who know the weakness of the enemy as well as they do our own dynamic resourcefulness. We have nothing to fear but our own unwillingness to let the issue be joined. And for a nation of salesmen this is a surprising limitation.

What could be more absurd, for example, than the pompous Communist propaganda that the empty doctrine they offer to a weary and impoverished world is either original or revolutionary? Or that Marx, Lenin, and Stalin were prophets who proclaimed a new social order?

Revolutionary? What is novel about tyranny? Since that remote day when the first caveman went round the intervening rock and successfully clobbered his neighbor because he was stronger and carried a bigger stick, evil men have oppressed the weak. The so-called Communist revolution brought nothing to the world but the reincarnation of old wrongs.

We must expose this fraud, and declare to all mankind that the real revolution in human affairs is the lucent, dynamic concept of the dignity of man, of freedom for the individual, which finds its fullest expression here in the United States. The end of tyranny — not its perpetuation — is our contribution to history.

We must not stop there, however. That is only the first plank in our platform.

If we would permit ourselves to study this alien philosophy thoughtfully, we would probably have to admit that, theoretically at least, Communism could exist as a social order apart from tyranny. It is conceivable that a new nation, formed by honest men who had surveyed the way of life in each of the other states, could adopt Communism by the full exercise of democratic procedures and voluntarily live by its ideas.

They would be wrong. But if we are to hold our own in the cosmic debate now going on in the remote areas of the world, we need to know *why* they would be wrong. We aim to permit each citizen to achieve the utmost fulfillment in his own life of those objectives which he himself has chosen.

All this we have done superbly.

The purpose of our production is to free the individual for the pursuit of the good life as he sees the good life. And, in retrospect, what we have achieved is incredible. No other social order yet conceived by man can match what we have done.

Our gross national product has passed the level of five hundred billion dollars per year, for a nation of one hundred and seventy-five million people, and it is doubling every twenty-two years. In the statistical period of fourteen years since the passage of the Federal Employment Act, employment generated by the people themselves, and not artificially created by the state, has advanced, on the average, by nearly eight hundred thousand a year, while the nation's output of goods and services has increased by more than 50 per cent. What could be more revolutionary than that?

When we reflect upon the crowded living quarters — intolerable by American standards — which are the lot of most Soviet workers, let us remember that in this same period we have built fifteen million new private non-farm dwelling units, and that 60 per cent of all non-farm dwelling units are owned by those who live in them. What shall it profit a nation to shoot the moon if four families must double up in a single apartment?

The more we can learn about what goes on inside Russia, the better we will be able to document the superiority of our system. By our standards, and when measured against the physical comfort and durable satisfactions of their people, the Soviets have devoted a disproportionate amount of their gross national product to missile development and grandstand plays in the field of astrophysics.

We never hear the Kremlin boast of the number of new automobile registrations. Not even they would dare do that, for the most casual visitor invariably reports that Russian streets and highways are barren of traffic. Only the élite, only the privileged in their class-less society, have private cars. There are no parking lots outside the steel plant at Magnitogorsk, and no two-car garages in the Moscow suburbs.

In fact, there are hardly any suburbs in our sense. Mr. K. made it quite clear, when he was in this country, that by concentrating working families in huge agglomerations of utility apartments near their place of employment, he could save for the state the vast sums which we "waste" on automobiles and roads. Fine for the state — but what about the people?

We should tell the world, too, that our tremendous surge of increased volume in production has been accompanied by an ever-widening distribution of the benefits of production and the responsibilities of ownership. Ingenious as the Communist technicians have been, there is one great invention which they have missed: they neither discovered nor copied our stock exchange. The share of stock, as evidence of private ownership and individual participation in a great enterprise, is still safely Western.

Our corporations now have about 12.5 million direct shareholders. And if we consider the stock held by pension trusts, insurance companies, and the like, it is probable that over fifty million Americans participate directly in the earnings of our industry. Most large companies now have more stockholders than employees, and by the same token, each year more and more employees become stockholders.

That, in my view, is the most astounding economic revolution in all history. What nonsense, what effrontery to hurl the vulgar epithet "monopolists" at us! What empty boasting to claim that Communists discovered the principle of the people's ownership of the means of production!

Or compare the two systems in accumulation of the capital required to add to the means of production, which further raises the standard of living. What is so novel about the method employed by the Communists? Under their social order, the state merely appropriates to itself the surplus which it requires — taking it away from those who have made the effort, without their consent. In the United States, each employed person makes his own decision as to whether he will consume or save. If he chooses thrift, he then makes another individual decision as to what form of investment he favors. The infinite multiplicity of these decisions makes up the force which determines the direction our economy will take. It is ours — not theirs — which is the true "People's Democracy."

The same difference is found when we compare the Communist system of education with that in a free America. Everything that we do in our schools and colleges is designed to benefit the individual; everything that they do is designed to benefit the state. We try to make it possible for all boys and girls to choose the intellectual discipline which will best suit their

talents, as they themselves see those talents, to the
end that their lives may be enriched as they advance
toward the objectives which they themselves formulate. Not so with Communism. The state determines
who shall be a scientist, a lawyer, an artist, or a nurse.
If a wrong decision is made, the individual is irrevocably committed to a lifetime of frustration. No
escape mechanism is available. This in itself must be
a great loss in effectiveness, even for a collective regime. I once knew an apothecary who ultimately became president of a great corporation. In Russia he
would have rolled pills and done nothing else till the
day of his death. How clear it is that ours is the dynamic way, and theirs the unenlightened!

There is one thing on the positive side to be said
about Communism. They are not afflicted with our
weakness: they are not afraid to study our system.
Soviet libraries undoubtedly contain many authentic
works on capitalism, and there can be no doubt that
Soviet economists keep abreast of current American
writing in the field of trade and production. When
they engage in dialectics with visiting American businessmen, it is they, not we, who are the better informed.

There is hope for the future in that, even against
their will, they are being driven by implacable economic circumstance to move away from their basic
philosophy toward ours. Karl Marx must be spinning

rather violently in his grave these days. "To each man according to his need, and from each man according to his ability" is steadily giving way to reward proportionate to effort. The direct application of the principle of incentives is spreading rapidly throughout the Communist industrial system. In the large plants, at least, the whole unit receives a bonus for output in excess of quota, and within the organization the particular departments have their own group quotas and bonuses. There is also an astonishing spread between the salaries and perquisites that are assigned to the various echelons of authority.

Even with respect to home ownership, there are signs of a crack in their brittle concept of collectivism. It now appears that one of the inducements offered in recruiting workers for new plants in the far reaches of Siberia, where until recently no man has ever gone voluntarily, is the privilege of building or buying a home that may be retained as private property.

Conceivably, too, the production commissars are being compelled to move crudely toward the basic elements of a price system and cost accounting. In their nationwide production line, as a commodity moves from one plant to another for further processing — such as steel to a tractor factory — there obviously has to be some basis for crediting the first plant with output and charging the next with intake.

Otherwise the bonus scheme would break down. You have to have a cost to start with if you are to measure the value of the added effort.

Similarly, in the field of foreign trade there has to be at least the crude outline of a price structure, particularly for buyers who deal with both West and East and want to make comparisons. The leaders of proud and highly nationalistic new nations are prone to the suspicion that other countries get a better deal. Communist traders know that to make a better proposition to India than to Burma is not a good way to win friends and influence people.

None of this is meant to suggest for a single moment that Communism is not still a great threat to world peace and to world economic stability. Quite the contrary. In the field of economic penetration the Soviets are tough, resourceful competitors. To hold our place in the world will require strong effort. But there is no cause for panic. They are no supermen. We can beat them, and on our own terms, if we will only fear them less and trust ourselves more.

One lesson we must learn from them, however. We must come to see as clearly as they do what it is that we believe, and must bring to the fulfillment of this revolutionary industrial faith of ours the same dedication of spirit and the same tirelessness of effort that they display in propagating theirs.

16

The Myth of Retirement

*Should key executives be retired at the peak
of their powers? Can companies afford
to lose the day-to-day guidance of
seasoned managers, solely because they've
reached a certain age?*

L ET THERE be no mistake about one thing: retirement itself is no myth.

Those of us who have already retired can certify to
that in full. Not a day begins but what we are keenly
aware of the change that has come into our lives. And
the change is good.

Retirement comes to each man in turn, except, of
course, to those few mad characters who behave as
though in their cases Providence, with infinite far-
sightedness, has suspended the rules and bestowed
upon them the priceless gift of executive immortality,
lest the world suffer disaster by having their steady
hands withdrawn from the control levers.

It is not the fact of retirement that is the myth, but
the reason why. The fundamental necessity for this
complete transformation in a strong man's life is badly

misunderstood and so clouded with fog that the cool, fresh wind of clear thinking is needed.

The first point which should be driven home to all concerned — and that means wives and children, as well as the general public — is this: In a large company, compulsory retirement is solely a function of organization morale and discipline. It has nothing whatever to do with the physical fitness or mental alertness of the individual concerned.

Selective retirement — the choosing of some to stay on when others are handed the gold watch of dismissal — cannot be wisely and fairly carried out as policy for a large group. The lawyer, the doctor, or the otherwise self-employed may make his own decision in this critical matter, but not the man who is responsible for the well-being of a fine institution. There just has to be a rule — and all must be governed by it.

Come sixty-five, or whatever the predetermined age, there are many fine Americans who are not only altogether fit but are actually at the very peak of their powers. Some at seventy, seventy-five, or eighty, look young, act young, and in fact are young. Superficially, it seems wrong to deprive a company of the great abilities of such men.

But that is only one side of the picture. Offsetting these paragons there is, unhappily, in every company a less favored group. These are the men who at sixty, or even less, have so slowed down that they no longer pull their weight. Such officers do more than block the advancement of abler, younger men. Because through seniority they have reached top responsibilities, the lethargy exercises a braking action on the entire corporation.

To choose those who should retire in these two contrasted groups may appear simple, but in practice it is complex, and utterly destructive to sound human relationships. Always there will be one or two on each side who are easily recognized. Everyone admires good old Charlie, who stands straight as a ramrod and never looked better. On the other hand, everyone feels sorry for poor old Fred, who has had so much sickness and trouble in his life that he is just going through the motions of working. In between, however, there are a lot more about whom opinions differ.

The youngsters think all the older men ought to quit. Those who are approaching retirement think they all look good.

Who is to choose? Who is so all-wise that he dares to look the whole company in the face and say this man shall stay and that man shall go? What doctor or psychologist has such all-pervasive understanding of the human body or of the human mind that he can devise reliable tests to determine fitness, so that management itself may be relieved of making the choice?

Even if such a miracle were to come to pass, the very giving of the tests would itself disturb morale. The man concerned would, of course, be the last person capable of forming a sound judgment about his own retirement. And so swiftly does change come in the later years that the testing would have to be almost continuous, and carried out at frequent intervals.

Each of us secretly believes that he is the genuine superman. If the test should be unfavorable, the individual in question would most certainly be grievously offended, and so would all his friends. Each dismissal would bring a flood of recriminations, rumors, and backstage gossip about the injustice done to those retired and the favoritism shown to those kept on.

Good team play cannot survive such tensions. Capriciously to release some men who have given long and faithful service while retaining others whose careers have been in parallel sets up stresses within an administration structure which wise management cannot tolerate. There must be a single standard and a single rule, one which is rigidly enforced without fear or favor.

As to what age retirement should be made compulsory, opinions may differ. Obviously it should approximate as closely as possible the median line between the more fit and the less fit. The judgment must be arrived at conservatively, and doubts must be resolved in favor of the company rather than of the individuals. At present, experience and common consent have placed the line at sixty-five years, but future generations of management men must from time to time review the question in the light of their own experience. The important thing is that there be a rule.

The man at the top must necessarily set the example. No matter how able at retirement age, he must nevertheless scrupulously apply to himself the rule by which he governs others. All right-thinking men know this and conform, but, incredible as it seems, there are still some petty tyrants who do just the opposite. Cads and cowards that they are, they so abuse the power given them that they retire subordinates while still keeping themselves on the payroll.

By way of parenthesis, it should be pointed out that the rule should govern executives, those who make the day-to-day decisions, as distinguished from those who serve on a board of directors, either of their own or of some other company. The qualities of fitness required are not the same in these two categories. After the time when a man should release to younger minds and wills the function of saying a crisp yes or no, there may well be a further interval when his wisdom and experience can have great value in the senior councils of his company. But here again there must be a rule which applies to all. Nothing is more embarrassing or pathetic than the struggle some corporations have to go through in trying to lose rich but senile directors. Present experience seems to indicate that seventy-two is about the right age at which to draw that line.

Let me repeat, however, that the establishment of these rules, whether for executives or for directors, is entirely disassociated from inquiry into the fitness of a particular individual. It is here that the mythology should be swept away, once and for all.

Retirement should carry no stigma of unfitness whatsoever. It should never be thought of as a life sentence to inactivity. It should be recognized as acceptance of a principle that bears upon the group welfare of the company, but one that has no bearing at all upon the man's own capacity to go on giving useful service to society.

Quite the contrary. Retirement may open up the most richly rewarding experience of a man's entire life.

Almost immediately, an exhilarating new freedom is bestowed upon him. In the life of every businessman there are things which he does, and does well, solely from a sense of duty, not because his heart is in them. The old obligations, which may have long since lost their novelty, no longer fetter him. He may now choose for himself the activities into which he will throw his energies, and not have the choices forced upon him. He may now seek out the new challenges which have long been in his mind, but which have been denied him because of the pressure of his routine duties.

Pity the man who has no unfinished business in his life, nothing that he has long dreamed of doing but which has been blocked off by the earnest business of making a living for himself and his family.

Could anything be sadder? At retirement his friends tell him that he should take up a hobby. What a loathsome word that is, carrying the connotation that desperate measures must be taken to keep the poor fellow from cutting his own throat! Surely his company can say "Good riddance" when he retires, for his self-starter has obviously long since ceased to function! A man so lacking in imagination and will power that he can think of nothing to do has probably not brought a new idea to his job in twenty years.

The man who cheerfully accepts retirement and enters with genuine enthusiasm into the reorientation of his life has one further advantage. He can select from his deferred agenda the activity which excites him most, and he can also establish his own tempo and rhythm in doing it. He can work part-time or full-time as he pleases, and can alternate almost at will his periods of activity with those of rest and relaxation. When the time comes for a vacation trip, he does not have to tell his wife that the company cannot spare him just then. He can take a series of short assignments one after another, tackling one and licking it and then moving on to the next, or he can fix his eye on just one objective for the rest of his life. Always he will be moving at his own pace, and setting his own goals.

He can also fix his own compensation. If his life has been lived in a calling that is underpaid, he can now sell his services to the highest bidder and try to make some money. In a surprising number of cases, a man who needs to be gainfully employed earns more after retirement than he did before. He has known for a long time that he could do better on the outside, but his pension rights have kept him on the job. Now he can smile each day at the thought of that larger pay check.

On the other hand, if he is fairly comfortable and can maintain a standard of living that is reasonable in the light of all his circumstances, he can learn the sheer joy of unselfish public service, the deep satisfaction of doing a job just because it needs to be done. At every level of society the world cries out today for men who will dedicate themselves to the public good. Our way of life is in peril. How can a man who has

reaped its benefits do better than to work for its preservation? Somewhere there is a task suited to every
skill, an unsolved problem that can be mitigated by
the very type of ability which the retired executive
has already displayed in his company. He ought to
know where the right spot for his effort is, but if he
happens not to, there are many who will point it out
to him.

The die is cast, however, long before age sixty-five,
and this part of the myth needs clearing up, too.
Whether a man will be prepared psychologically
when his turn comes to face the challenges and enter
into the satisfactions of retirement is irrevocably determined before he reaches middle life. It is not at
sixty-five, but at forty-five, that the basic decisions are
taken. If before he is forty-five a man has found nothing that fires his imagination, nothing that arouses
his creative powers and that enlists his best efforts
but the daily shuffling of papers on his desk, he will
be a pathetic failure in retirement. If he has never
risen above his job and gone all out for some task
or cause totally unrelated to his business, he will be
a hopeless case at sixty-five, a perpetual problem to his
family and his friends.

But if all along his life has been overflowing with infectious enthusiasm for ideas and ideals that have their
roots in a world outside the routine of mere money-

making, he will go on as long as he lives, growing in usefulness to the world about him, just from sheer personal momentum. He will not have to learn to fish at a time when his arthritis hardly permits him to hold a rod.

There is an added bonus, too. The physical and intellectual activity thus generated, along with the *joie de vivre* which inevitably springs from it, will actually prolong his life at the same time that it deepens his satisfactions. Retirement is challenge and excitement, not inaction; privilege, not abnegation.